"Divorce is one of the most difficult of human experiences. Psychologically and emotionally, divorce is a series of little deaths: the death of self-images, the death of a fantasy about how life was supposed to have been lived, the death of youthful hopes and dreams. To successfully navigate the journey of divorce without tripping on the many land mines... Donna Martini has provided us with a road map... triumph. With her wisdom and experience she ... ng her 'commandments' will be a remarkable t... for all those whose souls are injured from divorce."

Rabbi Perry Netter, author of *"Divorce Is A Mitzvah"*

PRAISE FOR DONNA

"There aren't enough words to express who this woman truly is. God has sent us one of his top Angels. Donna pulled me from the depths of the lowest point in my life and has shown me and my family a way to consistent and true Happiness." C.

"Donna has the unique ability to "connect" with those around her in a way unlike you have ever experienced before. She is experienced, dedicated, high-energy and without question "The Real Deal". R.

"It is difficult to describe the pure energy that Donna exudes and the sincere caring for everyone she touches. Without Donna and her influence I would not be the person I am today." M.

"Donna brings out the best in everyone she comes in contact with. It is all tied to her never-ending willingness to give and never give up on the people she feels are good, but maybe just lost for a moment in time. It is her gift." V.

"Donna Martini is no longer the best kept secret because she is out! D is a brilliant coach. She has transformed so many lives and now she can reach out to so many more with her writings. I am her biggest fan!" C.

"I met Donna at a low point in my life, but she helped me transform back and beyond my former self. Through the physical, mental, and spiritual, she taught me to take control and live life to the fullest. I now approach everything in a positive way!" R.

"It is rare to find someone that has so positively affected so many lives." S.

THE
TEN

how to leave your marriage

COMMANDMENTS

without breaking up your family

OF DIVORCE

DONNA MARTINI

ISBN-10: 0615470564
ISBN-13: 9780615470566
Library of Congress Control Number: 2011905161

Edited by John Kominicki
Cover and Illustrations by Michael Albano
Photography by Irene Andreadis
Printed in the United States

DEDICATION

*To my children, **Matthew and Heather:***
You gave me the motive
to become healthy,
and through loving and raising you,
I have become a better person.

*To my mother **Barbara:** Because without your*
support, nothing would have been possible.

*And finally, to the **father of my children:***
Through the practice of loving you, I have come to the
place I am today, and for that, I am grateful.

Acknowledgements

This book could not be written without the help, advice, and patience of the following people:

Jessica, my beautiful daughter-in-law: You picked up where I had to leave off.

John Kominicki, my brilliant editor: You challenge me to be a better writer.

Mary Lou, my dearest friend: You listened every day to every story without judgment.

Marie Amato, and Dottie Brandt, my prayer team: I feel safe because of you.

Nana, my incredible grandmother: You are an inspiration.

Perry Netter, my Jewish counsel: Your input and guidance was invaluable to me.

Vincent Amato, the source of many of my lessons about myself: Your support made this possible.

A special thank you to all of my contributors and content editors:

Alycia W LaGuardia
Grady Wallace
Honorable Elaine Jackson Stack
Michael C Savino
Richard LaGuardia

What You Should Know Before Reading this Book

It is never easy to hear what you may not be ready to heed. You have picked up this book, however, which means there is a part of you that is prompting a healing.

As a coach, I have made it a rule to only tell a client what I feel they need to hear, on a spiritual level, and not what I want to say. Not only can it be harmful to say too much, but it can cause a pushing energy, which is the exact opposite of what I want to accomplish. Your journey, in other words, is important to me!

To that end, I've written **The Ten Commandments** in segments, with each chapter its own separate entity, much like the Bible, so you can jump and skip around, start from the back, the middle, or the beginning. I want you, the reader, to take what you need at your own pace.

Book I is the "How to" of accomplishing the commandments. It sets you up, so to speak, and prepares you for the undertaking ahead. If this is where you start, and you can get through it, the rest of the book will be much easier to understand. If you start elsewhere, know that it will all make sense when you are done. On my journey, I have always tried to follow my gut, use my head and listen to my heart. It is my hope for you that by using your inner guide, you will extract exactly what you need at the moment you need it.

With warm regards, D.

CONTENTS

INTRODUCTION

'TIL DEATH DO YOU PART

Throughout this book, you will be led and guided to handle your divorce in a healthier and more spiritual way through a process I call *Positive Manipulation*. You will be asked to transmute your pain, anger, anxiety and fear into love energy that stems from a higher part of yourself. You will be prodded to think before you act and speak, and most especially, you will be asked to manipulate every negative notion you may have generated in your relationship with your ex. Yes, I said relationship, because no matter what, if you have children, you will need to co-exist on this Earth (with the very person you have decided to detach from) until the day you die.

Please know that I am not asking you to forsake or bury your negative emotions towards your former partner. Everyone needs and deserves time to grieve, to be angry, sad or disheartened. After all, even though all parties are still living, there has been a death in the family – the death of a marriage. Disregarding your emotional pain can cause disease in your body and your life. I am asking you to take on those negative emotions in a constructive way that will help you heal yourself and create a loving atmosphere for you and your family to live in. The task you are undertaking is enormous, self-sacrificing, and at the very least, difficult and challenging. You may feel unaided and without the support of the religious entity that married you, but no matter what your faith, there *is* a religion or doctrine of goodness you can adopt. Call upon your previous teachings and the love energy that led you to marry in the first place, and follow me while I introduce you to a new set of Commandments written expressly for this situation.

SCHOOL OF HARD KNOCKS

Going in, you should know I am not a doctor, nor do I have any initials after my name that would signify a degree in the sciences. I am a divorcee who has survived and moved on to thrive, which is the main point of reference from which this book comes. But I've also dedicated my life to coaching and helping people find – or as I like to say, *get out of* – their own way, which has given me a unique perspective and a certain kind of specialized training. It is through my clients that I am continuously graced and gifted with knowledge I wouldn't have been able to acquire on my own. Although there were some ethereal forces at work guiding the formation of the words you are about to read, my singular purpose is to change peoples' minds about our potential as humans and to open eyes and ears to the possibility of a new paradigm of divorce we can adopt and follow.

My biggest concern while writing this book was that I would have to reveal some hurtful things about my own marriage in order to be taken seriously. In other words, I would need to "trash talk" my ex. Is there really a need to show what I have gone through in order to prove how far I have come? My hope is no. My lessons might be marginally clearer with personal detail, but I hope you will understand my decision to remain silent for the sake of my children, their father and, most importantly, my need to follow the Commandments! At the same time, I don't want you to spend the next 200 pages with a *"Yeah, that's easy for her to say"* attitude, either.

Suffice it to say, I spent many years before and after the divorce living in fear, shame, anger, guilt and confusion. Irrespective of what you hear or don't hear about my circumstances, please don't discount the value of the information you are receiving. It's a punch bowl of poignant ingredients you can dip into and drink from. Please understand that no matter how awful *your* situation is, or who or what you are up against, you can still empower yourself and your children to create a more peaceful existence. Conveying your potential is my challenge. I only ask that you go in with an open mind so we can resolve these negative issues together.

"God offers to every mind its choice between truth and repose. Take which you please – you can never have both."
– Ralph Waldo Emerson

In order to initiate the Commandments, there has to be some acknowledgement. At one point, we all have to ask ourselves, "What is there about me that brought both the marriage and the break up?" Most of us won't admit to having much liability in the *getting there,* the ruination of our marriage, but if we don't take responsibility for changing what it is about ourselves that got us to this point, we will probably do it again. Studies from the Furstenberg, Peterson, Nord and Zill Life Course tell us that half of all American children will witness their parent's breakup. Of these, close to half will also see the breakup of one or more of their parent's second marriages. In any scenario, whether you are on your first, second, or third, it is time to create new objectives: To learn from the past, to live a harmonious life now, and in the future, to be able to look back and realize a successful job as a parent with no regrets.

"The gem cannot be polished without friction, nor man without trials." – Confucius

This book is about love and the compassionate energy it carries with it. It promotes accountability and responsibility for the paths we have chosen, as it teaches forgiveness, empathy, kindness and how to lead by example. It is about the need to empower our children so they can cope with *our* life decisions that affect *their* lives. It is about being happy to "do the right thing" no matter how much pain you are in, and when I seem to get tough, know that I am speaking for that small voice inside us all that beckons goodness and so desperately wants to be heard.

When you decide to listen to that influence and allow your best foot to come forward, know that it is followed by much power and energy from the Universe and from those of us that have been through it as well. We are all connected, and there is much truth and wisdom out there. When your ears and heart are open, you will receive. If you are a divorcee who is dealing with an unreasonable co-parent, I am with you and understand your woes – but you are still accountable. You may be your child's only connection to reality and the one stabilizing force they will ever know. In my view, if at least one parent can maintain the goodness through the tough times, leading by example, the children will come through with strength and grace. If both parents fall victim to negativity, the kids may not stand a chance of becoming well-adjusted adults who can have healthy relationships. The old adage, "two wrongs don't make a right" applies here. Whether you are just starting out or are years into your divorce process, it is never too late to bring in positive energy. You made the decision to marry, and for whatever reason, it didn't work. Now you made the decision to divorce. For the sake of the kids, let's make sure it's done right.

PROLOGUE

The "rude awakening" came late one night just a few months after the separation.

I was in bed, restless and very aware of the empty space next to me. Sleep seemed impossible, and with no one there to spoon with or share a hug, I decided to get up and seek the comfort of my 4-year-old daughter's room. As I walked in, the sight of curly, blond hair spilling over white sheets stopped me in the doorway. The moon's light was making her head shine with a halo, and I slanted a smile thinking about how angelic sleeping children can appear. I tip-toed in, adjusted the linens, as all moms do, and then knelt down beside the bed. Her breathing had a soothing rhythm, and I found myself resting my chin on the mattress so I could listen and follow.

As I studied her tiny features looking for signs of stress, I wondered if her dreams were peaceful. It was a simple notion, but it caused a shiver that left me with a disheartening thought—if this separation has made me feel so alone and isolated, so completely unsettled I found it difficult to sleep in my room by myself, how must she feel? I tugged at the ear of the teddy bear she had tucked tightly under her arm and realized it was her only night-time companion since birth. Could she be as lonely and scared as me?

And that was when it came. There was no lightning bolt or room shaking, no othe real voice from above, but there was an indisputable shift. My body was still mine, but my emotions were not. I felt the chill of her isolation, and my heart pumped with the fear, anxiety, and guilt that only a child of divorce could know. I fought the urge to climb into bed and comfort my little girl, lay my cheek next to hers and wipe the tears away, but I realized they weren't hers... they were mine. Somehow I was being allowed to experience her emotions. Somehow I became her, if only for a moment. But that was all it took.

When parents separate, they are so wrapped up in their own emotional turmoil, they sometimes don't realize how incredibly troubled the kids become. We put a roof over their heads, feed them, and make sure their surroundings are sound. We may get them into therapy, naively make statements like "everything is going to be alright," and then send them off to school as if their perception of a normal life were somehow still intact. We split up their home and send them packing every other weekend to sleep in a new bed without grasping how dramatically their universe has changed. We know on an intellectual level what we are putting them through, but do we ever try to *become* them, to really get into their heads and hearts?

Up until that point, I was more concerned with making money and holding it together so I could organize the day-to-day workings of my new single-parent household. I wasn't really considering how divorced my son or daughter must have felt. After all, wasn't I the one whose world was rocked, who lost a surname, contact with most of my friends, and was going from couple to single? The truth is I never realized my children had a new status as well. There wasn't a name or title for them, however; nothing to signify the change in their lifestyle. We don't actually acknowledge kids in that way. I am a divorcee, but what do we call them? Society sometimes uses the phrase "products" of divorce, as if they were manufactured goods waiting to be distributed.

That night, in the serenity of Heather's room, with only the moon as my witness, I had my epiphany, that 'aha' moment that allowed a new perspective, and I embraced it. I wasn't just a mother to my kids; I was their family, a huge part of their world, and a link to the unknown that was unfolding day to day in their short-lived but significant lives. Without me, where was their maternal guide? Without me and my leadership, each one might very well become a "product", a product of what the outside world wanted to make of them.

It was time to understand the significance of the culmination of my eggs and his sperm. No, the Earth wasn't supposed to revolve around me and my woes. Instead, it was meant to orbit around the incredible creations God decided to put here. As man-made as my marriage and divorce were, Heather and Matthew were not my products, and as privileged as I was to give birth to them, these children were not mine to ruin.

BOOK I

GAINING PERSPECTIVE

"They do not love that do not show their love. The course of true love never did run smooth. Love is a familiar. Love is a devil. There is no evil angel but Love."

– William Shakespeare

Chapter I
In the Beginning...

Saying "I Do," Then "I Don't"

Most of us say "I Do" with a love filled heart, offering it to our intended, wrapped in a bliss that is tied in yarns of hope and good intentions. We walk humbly through the doors of some sort of sacred structure and a formally dressed religious leader helps us announce to God, family and friends our undying commitment to love and honor "till death do us part." Unfortunately, as some of us leave our marriages, the gift of love unravels and the spiritual sentiment of our union flies out the window of that same building. When it comes time to say, "I Don't," the clergyman is replaced with an attorney and the religious structure converts into a courtroom. Hope is replaced with despair as the love turns to envy, disgust and, often times, hatred. Why do we enter into marriage one way and leave another? What makes us turn to God when we create a family, but turn to a judge when we want to break it up?

After witnessing the demise of many marriages, including my own, I have come to believe that the most detrimental aspects of divorce are the negative manipulation of one's own emotions and the loss of spirituality and divine direction. As we leave a partner, we begin the process most often by denouncing our original affection towards them. How many of us have heard the dreaded words, "I don't love you anymore?" In the state of mind that some separating couples create for themselves, there is the need to change the once-felt love energy into dislike or even total hatred so each can make the final "break." The need to change the emotion of love is a human tool used for self-preservation, but unfortunately, it acts like an ax that chops away at the heart and creates a complete split of our spiritual attachment to one another. Believing there is a necessity to stop loving our co-parent perpetuates the division of American families and is the biggest mistake we make as a society. Fortunately, it isn't impossible to repair.

Since the divorce process is so detrimental to all involved, we should be more inclined to leave the love in, *positively manipulating* the romantic aspects we once had into a purer, more altruistic sentiment the entire family can benefit from. We need to seek ways to keep the good parts of a marriage intact, utilizing the same spiritual sentiment and love energy we were wedded with to help keep the family bond strong long after we leave the marriage.

WHAT WERE WE THINKING?

Whether it was held in a church, temple, or erected altar and your union was officiated by a priest, rabbi, or some other religious or judiciary official, suffice it to say, you entered into marriage with more than just a license. There were commitments and pledges, optimism and soulful sanguinity. Most of us wanted God involved and we were willing to go through a lot of pomp and hoopla to get him there. Only a tiny handful of people will ever admit to getting married *knowing* and anticipating it would lead to a separation. The vast majority trust it will be forever, even though the statistics on divorce are staggering, and we all recognize that going in. We make the decision to marry irrespective of those odds, believing it won't happen to us. Or do we? Is there a mental escape clause we as humans use to deal with the enormity of our decision to wed? Do we go in thinking our marriage can be disposable?

Perhaps we need more of an understanding of what *forever* means. Maybe a rewrite of the vows to make it abundantly clear that "I do" is supposed to mean for life: "In sickness and in health, for richer, for poorer, through pain and anguish, or trial separation and contemplation of divorce, I will love and cherish you until the day I am placed in my coffin." Sounds too unrealistic? Before you accuse me of not appreciating our right to become single again, understand that I am not denouncing divorce. I literally ran from marriage once my decision was made. I would never deny anyone the choice of freedom from pain. It was the best decision I could have made at that time. Instead, I am proposing that we divorce with the same hopes as we wed, vowing that the breakup will not cause the ruination of lives, but will actually give each partner and their families what they ultimately want after leaving. Namely, peace and the pursuit of happiness.

People should not have to give up their right to the rite of marriage either, even though 50 percent of us choose our partners unwisely and then are too human and ill-equipped to handle the subsequent relationship. Please know that I say this with courtesy, respect and a chuckle, since I am in this category with you. My qualm is not with those of us who may have hastily gotten married or lack the skills to be a committed till-death-do-us-part husband or wife; it is not in the decision to get divorced or married. My apprehension for myself and fellow divorcees is centered on being a parental partner, a struggling single mother or father trying to make the new family dynamic the best that it can be. We, as a group, are shaping the emotional future, for better or worse, of millions of young people in America and throughout the world. All of us must – must – be willing to change our opinion of how we should proceed during the act of divorce, else our children will be entangled and mangled in our poor judgment "till death do us part" from them.

THE LAST RESORT, OR IS IT?

A portion of my time coaching is spent trying to save marriages. That's not to suggest that there are people out there who are too hasty in their decision to divorce. Most couples feel they have no choice or lack the means to deal with their differences and unhappiness. They don't believe they have the ability to change the negative aspects of their relationship, and they usually blame the wrong reasons for their marriage becoming unhealthy. That is where I step in, because statistically, staying and working things out is the best recourse. According to the Institute for American Values, almost eight out of 10 couples who avoided divorce were happily married five years later.

Everything from hormones and the chemically ridden food we poison ourselves with to the environment, money and stress can contribute to the downfall of a relationship. We often blame it on a lack of love, not realizing that love is a decision. We claim "irreconcilable differences," not understanding the need to continuously forgive each other and ourselves. We cite infidelity as a leading cause, but we never look into how bio-chemistry plays a role in leading us astray. We complain of "cruel and unusual punishment" and fail to consider mental illness as part of our vow to stick it out "in sickness and in health."

Too often we are ready to jump ship without really investigating the underlying causes. Not because we want to get divorced, and certainly not because it is easy. Staying almost always seems harder than leaving. Rather, it's because we don't understand the options. To know how to save a marriage requires the skills of a psychoanalyst, bio-chemist, translator, coach, mediator, nurse, financial advisor and in some cases, addiction counselor. We just aren't equipped emotionally or intellectually to handle all the idiosyncrasies of the human persona – our own or that of our spouse.

Since we don't know how to fix each other's problems, we decide to depart, not realizing that leaving doesn't necessarily solve anything. When couples split, they are often amazed at how unhappy they still are! Clients who have been divorced for any length of time come to me with their tales of woe, and I listen as they walk me through their former marriage and subsequent relationships, all with pretty much the same outcome. When they are done, I ask, "Who or what is the common denominator in your life?" Ultimately, they come to the conclusion, "It's me." When the realization is made that it may not have been entirely the other person's fault, when the need to work on their own issues becomes clear, the real mending can begin.

After becoming single, there are so many new problems to pin misery on. Co-parenting issues, lack of money and living arrangements are a few, but many of the real reasons for discontent are still with us, or I should say, *within* us. As the German writer and spiritualist Eckhart Tolle puts it, *"They (intimate relationships) do not cause pain and unhappiness. They bring out the pain and unhappiness that is already in you."* Clearly, the issues that we need to heal from do not leave our personas as we physically leave a marriage. They follow us ... relentlessly.

To Be In or Not To Be In...Is That the Question?

Putting blame or reason aside, divorce is still a choice we are allowed to make. When separation becomes a reality with my clients, my first reaction is, "Do they know what they are getting into? Do they realize how difficult the divorce process is? Are they anticipating a fairy tale life awaiting them? Do they understand how traumatizing it will be on the family?" I gingerly ask, "It's your decision to be free, but what about the kids? How are you going to make their life *for better* now that you realize you can't handle the *for worse?*"

When a marriage doesn't work, we get out bodily, changing our status and names and address. But most of us stay the same as individuals, still lacking the set of skills we needed to make the relationship work. We focus on the lost love, new animosity, broken hearts, disintegrated assets and households turned topsy-turvy, but rarely on the need to remain civil enough toward one another to raise a healthy, happy family. It's certainly our right to get out physically, but shouldn't we also consider the need to stay *in* emotionally, and more importantly, spiritually?

Do Unto Others

While doing research for "The Ten Commandments" and trying to understand the lack of what I call "divine decorum" in the world of divorcing couples, I came across a wonderful book written by Rabbi Perry Netter. Perry's own breakup led him to seek answers through the Torah, where he found very little religious direction to help him on his journey. In addition, he found it difficult to council members of his temple who were coming to him looking for answers to their own divorce issues.

Although there is much in the Old Testament about how to act in a marriage, the rabbi gleaned only small tidbits about the divorce process. Fortunately, what he did find led him to a profound conclusion: that leaving a marriage should be deemed as sacred an act as staying in. The rabbi tells us how he was stunned while reading an excerpt offered by preeminent biblical commentator Rabbi Shlomo Yitzhaki, who lived in the 11th century and was best known as Rashi. *"On the biblical command to write out a bill of divorcement, he said, quite simply, 'divorce is a mitzvah.'"*

In simple Hebrew, a mitzvah is an act of kindness. Rabbi Netter, however, takes it a step further: *"A mitzvah is not merely a good deed. A mitzvah is a response to the voice of God commanding us to behave in a particular way. A mitzvah is an obligation. This, then, is what I believe Rashi was teaching us; just as marriage is initiated with certain and specific obligations in Jewish tradition, just as marriage is entered into with ritual acts and a legal document, known as a ketubbah, so too is marriage terminated with ritual acts and a legal document, known as a get. Marriage and divorce could not be more different in the way they are experienced, but Rashi teaches us that the painful in life has no less a requirement to be experienced with holiness than does the joyous."*

If you are part of any religion that follows Christ, a mitzvah would probably be considered the same as an act of Christianity. Yet, there is not much written in the New Testament about how a Christian should treat their former spouse during a divorce either. One could ask, "What would Jesus do?" and probably deduce that he wouldn't likely hide his assets or sue his ex for a reduction in child support. Unfortunately, there is little teaching in any religion that specifically speaks about how to behave after you leave your marriage.

IT MAY NOT BE ALL OUR FAULT

Considering how negatively divorce has been portrayed, even frowned upon throughout the decades, especially in the Catholic Church, perhaps it is not practical to think we could have kept spirituality in. Up until the 1990s, some people believed their church regarded divorce as a sin and that they were considered excommunicated as soon as they broke their marital vows. Many divorcees I've worked with or interviewed felt "pushed away" from their religion by shame and guilt. This is tragic, especially when you consider just how important spiritual direction is when someone is going through such trauma. Thankfully, these views have changed, but programs through religious organizations are slow to come. Some faiths have pre-marital classes, and also have help for those seeking healing in a relationship, such as Retrouvaille or Marriage Encounter and one-on-one or couple counseling with a spiritual director. Sadly, there is little spiritual instruction offered to co-parents on how to live harmoniously as a bi-nuclear family.

As children, many of us grew up in a system of religious teachings, spending countless hours in Hebrew class, Sunday school or Catechism, and we were taught to be pious and caring. Morals were embedded in our minds and hearts every Saturday and/or Sunday. But, when divorce encroaches upon a family, what entity exists out there that can teach us to be loving and generous toward our future ex? The court regulates much of what we must do monetarily, but who will guide us ethically? Where is the director or coach that will show us how to behave, especially in front of the children?

Everyone knows divorcing couples who are at odds in the court system over custody, money or living conditions. Society has conditioned us into thinking that divorce should be a declaration of war. Whether this has been perpetuated by the dueling divorcees, their attorneys, or both, doesn't matter, and it's not my argument to make. Irrespective of what created this inane "legal" behavior we have adopted, it must be changed. We can't afford – mentally, emotionally, or financially – to be hateful to one another or to allow a court system to be the only determinant in our family's future.

Instead, we must bring more consciousness into the process by tapping into our own innate sense of fairness and ability to generate goodness. Attorneys are brought in to apprise us of our rights and interpret the law. Mediators help settle legal arguments. Judges make sure that conclusions reached are fair and equitable. None of these officials wish to be your guiding light, or conscience, and we have already agreed religious counsel is hard to come by. We ourselves must make divorce into a Mitzvah, an act of kindness, and a spiritual endeavor by going back to our original desire to love and honor. Only then can we leave the marriage with as much grace, respect and spirituality as we went into it with.

THE BEST WAY ISN'T ALWAYS THE EASY WAY

If you listen to Richard Dawkins, the noted scientist and author of the groundbreaking book "The Selfish Gene," he would have us believe that we are not hardwired for altruism. Instead, he proffers, *"Be warned that if you wish as I do to build a society in which individuals cooperate generously and unselfishly towards a common good, you can expect little help from biological nature. Let us try to teach generosity and altruism, because we are born selfish."*

Although he admits to not having a clear-cut, permanent solution to society's dilemma, he does agree that we can change, hence my desire to write this book about manipulating our own energy. Dawkins may never use the term **Positive Manipulation**, but we are both implying the need for a process. There is a necessity to continually go against our human tendencies in order to do what is right. It takes a great deal of energy to go against our own genes, nevertheless, what is our alternative? Isn't it much harder to live in constant turmoil than to try to generate peace by changing our own habits? If there were a set of rules you could follow that would ensure a successful divorce – and by that I mean, both parties end up relatively okay, no one is destitute, and most importantly, the children feel secure and loved by both parents – would you live by them? Have you made it your goal to come out stronger, more loving and a better person for having been married in the first place? If you said yes to any or all of these questions, then you are well on your way towards a great divorce.

CHAPTER 2
WHAT IS POSITIVE MANIPULATION AND HOW DO WE APPLY IT?

THE DEFINITION

Often listed as one of the five most stressful events in life, divorce is by far the most long-term situation in which one must apply a ***Positive Manipulation*** process. So what do I mean by putting the two words *positive* and *manipulation* together? Its definition – and trust me, you won't find this in Webster's – is to physically, emotionally, mentally and spiritually convert the negative energy within us and around us into its most positive form.

Look up "manipulation" in any dictionary and you will see the words "manage" and "handle." Used in certain contexts, it doesn't have to have a harmful connotation. In fact, if I were to hand you a piece of clay and ask you to manipulate it into the shape of a dog, you wouldn't hesitate, understanding exactly what I meant. Use it in any other circumstance, however, and it takes on a whole different meaning. So for most people, adding the word "positive" to "manipulation" seems to create an oxymoron. Throughout the years, I have taken much heat for the phrase from naysayers, who felt the two words should never be in the same sentence, let alone squeezed together as one phrase and trademarked! I've never faltered, though, and continue to maintain the words belong in concert.

Other writers talk about different processes of positive self-manipulation. Thomas Keating refers to self-transformation as conversion and calls the process "the contemplative journey". In his book "Think and Grow Rich," Napoleon Hill dubs it "voluntary self effort," and refers to the manipulating of one's own energy as "transmutation." Perhaps if Hill were alive today (he wrote the book in 1937 and died decades ago), he would have no issue using a word as provocative as manipulation. Or maybe transmutation is a more accurate vocabulary word. As genius as he was, I would not want to argue against his wisdom, so instead I humbly offer his teachings and juxtapose them to mine.

MANIPULATION IS NOT A DIRTY WORD

To make it more palatable to those people who cannot get past the negative connotation, you should know that *Positive Manipulation* is done to yourself, not others. When you encounter divorce, however, your first inkling is to protect, self-preserve and possibly negatively manipulate. If Dawkins is correct, that's only human. The last thought on anyone's mind is to give love and put their best foot forward. After all, putting your foot anywhere in the vicinity of your future ex may mean getting it lopped off!

Instead, consider the idea of every one, every thing, every situation you encounter, having an energy attached; an influence, positive or negative on your body, emotion, mind and attitude. Knowing that everything coming at you can be potentially deemed as either good or bad means you have a decision to embrace or release. It gives you cause to bring it in as is, or change it into what is appropriate to your needs or the needs of the moment. The act of *Positive Manipulation* is really an ability to take whatever is not working towards your goal and turn it into something worthwhile, that can attach to or radiate from a loving place within you. Whether it is for self-protection, or for an altruistic act you do for someone else, **Positive Manipulation** creates positive energy that can be felt immediately by you and those around you.

Hill put it this way: *"The secret of control lies in understanding the process of transmutation. When any negative emotion presents itself in one's mind, it can be transmuted into a positive or constructive emotion, by the simple procedure of changing one's thoughts."* Hill believed we could manifest anything through thought control, and it doesn't have to stop there.

IT'S ORIGIN

The term **Positive Manipulation** came to me many years ago at the onset of my separation in the early 1990s. It was a beautiful summer evening and I was walking with a neighbor, telling her about an issue I had with my husband. I can barely recall the details of that story, but I vividly remember her accusing me of manipulating him. "Well," I said resentfully, "if I am, it is a positive manipulation and it will benefit all of us in the end!"

At the time, I didn't fully appreciate the words I'd chosen, but as the months rolled on, I understood my indignation. I was twisting myself into a pretzel, using a manipulation process on *myself*, not him, trying hard to hold back every negative word and thought in order to maintain a healthy relationship with the father of my children. I knew how disrupted our lives had become because of the break up, and I was determined to create peace. What good was becoming a happy divorcee if my kids and their father were miserable? It didn't make sense to go from one state of turmoil to another, and somehow I knew love and forgiveness were the answer.

Now, I am making this sound easy, but it was not! The concept was innate, but the practice was tough. I was incredibly mishandled throughout my marriage and harbored plenty of pain and anguish. I had all the appropriate human reasons to hate and never forgive him, but I tried earnestly to let them go, thinking, "I'm done with the past and can start a new life. There will be no room in my heart for anger, especially if I fill it with love and forgiveness." As naïve as I was at the time about healing, I believe I was guided by common sense, a necessity to survive and, most importantly, love. My altruistic attitude didn't come from me being a saint. It came from me being a mother. And I wasn't being totally selfless. I was acting on behalf of myself as well. It was the only way to achieve my goal of living a happy life. I wanted what was best for the father of my children, but that wasn't my initial objective. Keeping him loving towards me was what I was after. It was the only way we would all survive the trauma, and I knew someone had to start the process. Armed with this selfless/selfish attitude, I was able to overcome many negative emotions I had towards him and the numerous uncomfortable situations our family was exposed to.

STARTING NEW

My *Positive Manipulation* practice instinctively began immediately after he left. Hoping not to make our situation worse, I tried to be as polite and gracious as I could. I found it relatively easy to be positive about the future though because I was so happy that the marital stress was gone. I was willing to forgive almost all of my negative emotions towards him since I knew he had a beautiful soul, even if it was temporarily masked by what I perceived as lots of negatives.

The first step I took was to create a goal, "I want to be the best person and mother I can be." The second step was to attach a motive to it: "Because I want my kids to be healthy and feel secure and loved." (Yes, there is a difference between a goal and motive, but more of that later.) This goal, with its altruistic motive, sent a force out into the universe that rippled for years. There wasn't a day that went by that I didn't feel angels around me and validation for what I was doing, not to mention a newfound strength and conviction. No matter what situation occurred, I was able to handle it, most often with a positive outcome.

Again, this is not to say that I always did the right thing. I am human and admit to it, but the conclusion of any episode we endured seemed to help and not hurt in the end. Like a cat, I always landed on my feet no matter how far I was thrown, taking any negative energy that was coming toward me and manipulating it into an energy I could use. Hate for what was done to me transformed back into love, anger turned to tolerance and forgiveness, anxiety became empathy, and fear evolved into a need to succeed and desire to learn – a quest for knowledge so strong it brought me to write this book. Ultimately, peace was kept and the children and I not only survived, we thrived.

I started out humbly, realizing that the true value in the goal/motive step is to start somewhere and continuously admit that I may not have any idea how I am going to make it happen. I have a quip I use all the time: "I am smart enough to know that I am not smart enough to know everything about anything." As soon as we let go of the idea that we know best, the best way to do things appears. I once read, "Nature abhors a vacuum." It took me a long time to figure out what that meant, but it is my understanding that when we clear ourselves of any ego issues, our heads become vacuous and the info and assistance we need comes right to us. This is a law the universe grants that you can always rely on!

THE SOUL OF THE MATTER

In order to recognize the need to *Positively Manipulate* ourselves, we first have to understand what we are comprised of. How do we choose the paths (right or wrong) that we ultimately embark on? When asked the age old question, "Who are we, and why are we here?" philosophers and theologians offer many plausible theories. With terms like the shadow, the ego, and the self, I have spent countless hours since childhood in a state of confusion trying to figure out who or what we are.

Being brought up Catholic, the Trinity had a profound effect on me. I was five years old when I began to question why I needed to take my hand from my forehead to my chest and then across. "Okay, I get that God is the father and Jesus is the son, but who is the ghost and what does holy really mean?" Many people take for granted the sign of the cross, but I never did. Wanting to thoroughly understand what it meant, I asked my mom. When I didn't appreciate her answer, I decided to go directly to God. As an innocent kid, I didn't think twice about God answering me, and eventually he did. It wasn't until many years later, though, that I understood the answer. Rene Descartes declared, *"Body and Soul are two distinct, separate entities entirely unrelated to one another,"* and I agree, to a degree. Okay, they can be split in two, but I further query, are they supposed to be?

YOU MAY NOT BE ALONE IN THAT BODY OF YOURS

No matter what religion you were exposed to, you have probably been taught that we are comprised of two entities, one being the human body and the other being a soul or spirit. When you begin to comprehend this, an amazing realization arises; we are not beholden to the body we come in. We can transcend all our shortcomings. We can let go of our physical selves and tap into an incredible power that could never be defined in human terms. Why? Because we just don't have the vocabulary yet to describe it. Recently, scientists have been disproving century old scientific "facts," realizing there may be a higher power or "force" yet to be discovered or identified. With movies like "The Secret," "What the Bleep Do We Know" and Dr. Wayne Dyer's new release, "The Shift," we are being challenged through quantum physics to look at ourselves in a completely new light. What is reality? What are we really capable of and who or what is out there that we can rely on to help us?

While growing up, I was aware of two personas I called "Big Donna/Little Donna," which were distinct and separate people in my head. Big had a loud voice and was first to respond. Little was tiny and a struggle to hear. I was in my late 30s when I began to fully understand what these voices represented. Thomas Keating says, *"Instead of trying to free us from what interferes with our ordinary human life, the Spirit calls us to transformation of our inmost being, and indeed of all our faculties into the divine way of being and act-ing."* He continues his explanation by adding, *"The Greek fathers called this process deification."* We all have an inner soul voice that is constantly beck-oning us to transform out of what our human selves have gotten us into. Since being human makes us flawed, so too are most of our thoughts and actions. At the time I discovered my two voices, I followed what was louder and stronger, irrespective of what it was telling me to do. The little voice didn't stand a chance and, in addition, the direction it was asking me to follow was difficult and uncomfortable. What I didn't realize was that as I got healthier and desired more love and positive energy in my life, the two entities switched. Now Little Donna became the new Big Donna, meaning the voice of positive reason was becoming louder and easier to follow. This was a huge step in my own growth. I realized that the volume was now controlled by what my intentions were, not what my human self wanted to hear!

We have heard of people doing extraordinary things. The "Spirit" within each of us is capable of much more than we ever use on a daily or even yearly basis. We can overcome anything we put our minds to. That incredible power that we call God or Buddha, Allah, Divine, Source, Jehovah, Great Spirit, exists within all of us, but do all of us make use of it? Do we listen to the source or forget it's there to tap into? Call me a complete novice in the field of religion, but I believe—and Gandhi agreed—that all of them have truth, and if you look closely and listen carefully, the majority promote one concept profoundly; to love and share of ourselves, the best of what we have to offer. Most of the rules, traditions, sacrifices, offerings, etc, can be categorized under the heading of grace, love, compassion, forgiveness and selfless acts. And the best examples we have are the stories given in the Torah, the Bible, the Tripitaka, the Tao, the Kabbalah – the list goes on.

Irrespective of how each of us interprets the Divine Plan described in our own religions, isn't it possible that we all share the same energy? And if we have been blessed with this ethereal power, aren't we then capable of chan-neling that same energy through our human selves? Famous leaders from all over the world, like Mohandas Gandhi, Sri Chinmoy, the Dali Llama, Martin Luther King, Rashi, Mother Theresa and others, have all promoted this concept. Many of us try to utilize these teachings, but most of the time we fall short, believing it is too difficult. Even Christians, who have the example of Jesus to follow, sometimes believe they need to be special and inordinately graced in order to accomplish what I put into one general category called **goodness**.

Positive Manipulation is the act or discipline of managing those voices within us. It is about making a case for doing and saying what is right for everyone and using our soulful, mindful ears, instead of our human ones. It is about talking ourselves out of what we really want to do in order to do what we really should do. It allows us to recreate ourselves so the spirit and goodness within us will constantly, easily, and joyfully be revealed. Our soul (as I like to call it, but please feel free to use your own word) is comprised of pure love energy, and we need to be reminded every minute of every day that we all have the ability to utilize it every minute of every day! Even if you don't believe in God, accept and embrace this higher consciousness because it is within you.

If you are reading this book, there is most likely a small voice inside beckoning you to turn up the volume so it can be heard. It wants you to know that you have the ability to lift yourself from your human bodies' frailties and occasional negative state of being just long enough to do what you need to do. Whether we decide to use it or not, we all have the potential to be our best selves and to emit, articulate, and transfer the love energy we were created with. It is called free will, but you should know, it doesn't come freely – unless, of course, you will it to.

"Making the decision to have a child is momentous.
It is to decide forever to have your heart go walking around outside your body."
Elizabeth Stone

CHAPTER 3
HEADING IN THE
RIGHT DIRECTION

THE GOAL AND THE MOTIVE

Reading this book, most especially if you have purchased it for yourself, is an indicator that you may already have made it a goal to prompt your best divorce. If that is so, do you know your actual motive? Do you recognize the difference between the two? *A goal is something you want to achieve, but a motive is the reason why you are doing it.* For instance, I started out my journey as a single mother wanting to have the best divorce possible and be the best mother I could be (goals) for the sake of my children (motive). At that point, I was so low in the self-esteem department I had trouble believing I deserved to have a better life for myself. Instead, I used my kids and the love I had for them to help me move forward in a positive light. On the first leg of your journey to finding your best self, you may not believe you have a strong enough motive to keep you going. Overcoming emotions like fear, guilt, anxiety, sorrow and anger are incredibly difficult and can hold us in limbo for many years if we allow them to. The motive we place behind our goal is the real energy or power, the oomph, we need to make our goal into reality. Without it, we may flounder aimlessly with no real direction.

In order to transcend your pain and angst toward your former partner and find the forgiveness you need to heal, you may *only* have the love for your kids as a precursor. That's okay! Use them! During the beginning stages of my separation, I had to actually fake it at times. In fact, there was a part of me that was so angry about how my life was being directed I thought it would consume me. I used anger as a weapon against love, giving me the strength and conviction I needed to leave. I remember so vividly during the end stages of the marriage how I would fantasize about hitting him with an iron skillet. This daydream ran like a DVD in my head as I vividly imagined myself creeping up from behind while he was standing in our kitchen making a sandwich. With two hands wrapped around the handle, I would wail him right upside his ear until he was down for the count. This little video I created relieved a lot of stress and made me feel empowered, but kept me embroiled in anger. Turns out, it wasn't only anger towards him – it was mostly towards myself. It was a mask I was using to cover the intense pain and hurt I felt about what my husband was capable of doing to me. Under the guise of love, his actions during the marriage mutilated my self-esteem and well-being, and I allowed it year after year. In order to survive the painful reality of that so-called love, I had to put on a false bravado of rage to feel strength and conviction.

The anger helped me survive, but it had to go in order for me to move on and be a good co-parent. It is a challenge to find that part of yourself that can give love irrespective of how much pain you are in, but it is initially *your choice* to make it a goal. Do so and your life will never be the same. And when you take on this challenge, understand that you don't have to know how to do it! That will come. All you need is desire and through that desire you will receive the methods, the means, the stamina and the universal knowledge you need to accomplish your goal.

THE FOUR ASPECTS OF BEING HUMAN

Now that we understand the two entities we are comprised of – the human body and the soul – and we know how to recognize and create both a goal and a motive, we can move on to the make-up of the human persona. In order to start the process of *Positive Manipulation*, there are four aspects to consider: the physical, the emotional, the mental and the spiritual sides of ourselves. All are equally important and all affect and trigger one another.

Most spiritual people assume that the soul energy is their true life force, but truthfully, it is only one part of one's being. Because we are encased in organic bodies that walk the earth, eat, drink, sleep and are held down by gravity, they have their own energy, and we are driven by them as well. Additionally, we have the personality to consider. In his book "Seat of the Soul," Gary Zukav explains, *"The World as we know it has been built without a consciousness of soul. It has been built with the consciousness of the personality. Everything within our world reflects personality energy. We believe that what we can see and smell and touch and feel and taste is all there is to the world."* When you consider all of this, how challenging does life become? We are potentially led by our body, mind, or persona, which may be influenced every minute by everything that is happening in and around us. Then we need to remember how molded and infected we are being exposed year after year to all kinds of harmful situations and chemicals, and holding on to all sorts of past emotions and traumas. It is scary to think of what energy is running our lives.

WHO OR WHAT IS DRIVING YOU?

When it comes to maintaining a straight path and listening to that higher part of you, there is the need to *Positively Manipulate* the negative that you may be physically and mentally encased in. After all, following the direction we are being led is as imperative as creating the goal itself. So understanding the energy that should be guiding us on our new journey is crucial. We have all heard of and used the term "free will," but do we fully understand what it is? My definition, simply put: It is the choice we make day to day, minute by minute, whether to follow our loud human voice or the softer-spoken, always-positive voice of our soul.

In his book "The Laws of Spirit," Dan Millman creates a character called the Mountain Sage who describes this concept beautifully: *"Free will means that you can choose to abide by the laws that speak within your deepest intuition, or you can let impulses, fears, and habits run the show. If you sometimes resist or ignore higher wisdom in favor of immediate gratification, the consequences of your choices eventually guide you back toward alignment with the laws of Spirit; one choice leads to a sunlit path and another to hurdles and tests that instruct and strengthen you, so all things serve in their own ways."*

To go back to my Big Donna/Little Donna scenario, I learned that when my body was right with the world and my intentions were positive, the stronger voice was that of my soul. On the contrary, when my body was a mess, broken and in a state of turmoil, the human voice was screaming way too loud for anything else to be heard, and that dictated my actions. At that point, I didn't have a positive intention behind what I said and did, only a negative reaction.

To make this concept simpler to understand, think of your human body as a car and your mind as the driver, and then imagine that soul energy or your own higher intelligence is your navigation system. Most often, we as humans have gone through a lifetime of trials and tribulations that allows us to be driven or compelled by a pretty negative driver in directions we don't necessarily want to go. The navigation system (our soul), however, has a much higher IQ. It's unaffected by its surroundings and is part of a huge GPS system, the universe, run by a computer we can't even come close to understanding. If we input a positive destination (altruistic goal) into that navigation system, we can allow it to guide us and it will take us where we want to go. Unfortunately, we don't always listen, doubting the ultimate wisdom it has.

If you have ever used a navigation device, how many times have you said, "that doesn't sound right!" and taken a turn against the "advice" spoken by the voice or direction it is showing? Thankfully, if you are wrong, the system puts you back on track every time, so even if you veer off the right path, you can always get back on, ultimately ending up at your desired destination. When we set a beautiful goal with an altruistic motive (which is the fuel for your car, by the way) such as, "I want the healthiest divorce for the **sake of my children**", we can't veer off course for long. No matter what inane, cruel, or unjustified human thing we might say or do, we are always guided right back by that higher power.

Our souls are motivated by pure love energy with no ulterior motive. And their voices are always positive and always right, but very often, just like our navigation, can't or won't be heard by a negative human body. We sometimes argue with it as if we believe the system is guiding us in the wrong direction, or worse, we turn it off and don't listen to it at all. That's quite a dilemma when you are trying to get to your best life (destination) and you have no idea how to get there.

Much of my research in the last decade has been with moods and how they are related to the foods that we eat and the biochemistry those foods create within our bodies. Through books like "Molecules of Emotion," written by Candace Pert of "What the Bleep Do We Know" fame, I have also learned that the chemistry existing within us forms a dynamic info network linking mind and body. This means that what we think about actually instigates our bodies to produce peptides, enzymes and cells to match that thought. So if you are constantly repeating a negative mantra to yourself over and over, your body is helping you become more and more determined to hold onto that negative philosophy. Even if you decide at a later date that you want to change your mind, your body has a hard time letting you do it! You can start to imagine now how many unhealthy aspects of us can be guiding and directing our decisions at any given moment.

CASE IN POINT: WHAT CAME FIRST?

I had a client named Harry who came to me recently, incredibly despondent over his separation. After spending very little time with him, it was
abundantly clear that he was not in his *right* mind and could never be with
his current lifestyle. Eating a ton of sugar to self medicate and drinking
coffee all day at work to keep himself going, he would arrive home in the
evening feeling alone and depressed. Each night he would toss and turn
agonizing over not being with his children and going over the reasons why
his wife tossed him out. After each sleepless night, he would go back to
work, drink more coffee and eat more sugar so he could function.

What Harry didn't realize was that these same eating and sleeping habits
caused the extreme intolerance and anger he felt towards his family when
he was married. Going home from work every day on a sugar low, he would
rant until his meal was served and then collapse on the couch in a "dinner
coma" until it was time to go to bed. Because he napped after dinner, he
couldn't fall asleep at night, so he would watch TV until he was bleary-
eyed. His body's negative state dictated his mind's concept of why he was
miserable, too, blaming his unhappiness on everyone from the government,
to traffic, his job, wife and kids. His mind (the guy at the wheel) was driving his family crazy because his body (the car) was fueled with chemicals
and polluted gas.

Harry had no goals, in fact, his navigation system wasn't even on, nor did he
realize he had one! And even if he were to find it and switch it on, it probably wouldn't be heard over the ramblings of what I call the "yappy dog" he
had in the back seat of his car, continually barking negative messages. Lucky
for him, some aspect of his persona asked for change. Perhaps his loneliness
instigated the realization that something had to give and that, in turn, triggered the chain of events that led him serendipitously to me.

Upon meeting him, the first thing I wondered was what came first – whether
it was his abuse of sugar (bodily cravings) or his attitude (emotional and

mental state) that led him to eat sugary foods in the first place? In the end, it didn't matter because we set out to change everything. All of it caused his separation, and although he started his healing process by coming to me for help, he must remain committed to altering the direction of his life permanently. Understanding that something is wrong is a great first step, but wanting to transform, to commit to change what isn't working, to be accountable for his actions and take full responsibility for the shape his body and mind are in, that's a lifelong progression.

If he starts the *Positive Manipulation* process and can cleanse his body of chemicals, his mind will clear, his emotions will change, and he will have the opportunity to see his life from a more realistic perspective that is not tainted by negativity. Only then will any form of therapy or counseling I lead him to be able to get him on the right road. Finally setting his navigation system to "find my best life" will be the biggest decision he ever made, and in his case, it may not be too late to get his family back – another goal he set soon after meeting me.

I have seen drastic changes in men and women when their diets are altered, and that is why I expend an enormous amount of energy, and pages of this book, describing the ill effects of having a negative or imbalanced body. Correct someone's biochemistry and they automatically become calmer, happier, clearer and less compulsive. I've seen marriages saved on this principle alone! Imagine how much better your existence as co-parents can be if both parties are physically healthy with balanced hormones and no toxicity in their systems?

> **"Are we human beings having a spiritual experience or spiritual beings having a human experience?" – Wayne Dyer**

After going through the process of eliminating negative energy in my body, mind and, most especially, my heart, and then coaching others to do the same, I have seen first-hand the amazing benefits. We can easily become a product of our own body instead of allowing our body to be driven by our more powerful soulful self. Please excuse the repetition here, but it is too important not to inculcate: Since we are human and walk the Earth with all of its potential for harm, we often allow our bodies and their sometimes negative state of being to lead and dictate our direction. Instead of listening for the voice inside of us that portends our greater purpose, and creating goals to accomplish that purpose, we let the way we think and feel at any given human moment guide our every move, usually leading us nowhere.

The good news is, no matter how negative we have become physically, emotionally, mentally or spiritually, we can transform ourselves and the negative energy using the many tools offered here. No matter how egregious our past was to our psyche and body, it is never too late to start and no condition is irreversible! In addition, we have four aspects to choose from. If one is unbearable to face, we can begin our journey transforming one of the others.

It has been my experience that you usually must begin your *Positive Manipulation* practice with the physical and mental aspects first, meaning, we accept the state our lives are in, take responsibility for where we are, set our goal, and then seek out anything physical that needs to change. Many may consider goal setting to be more spiritual, much like prayer. Creating and then speaking/writing the goal is utilizing the mental and human aspects, which stimulates spiritual energy. I believe we all start out earnestly wanting to be led by our spiritual side, but remember, we are usually being *controlled* by our body and its biochemistry. The question we should ask ourselves on the beginning of our journey is; "Which is stronger, my body with its cravings, addictions and skewed emotions and thoughts, or my soul's will to overcome them?" At any given time, one or the other is stronger. Sometimes we are oblivious to who has set the destination in our navigation system and, maybe worse, who has the wheel.

The concept of *Positive Manipulation* is always to *get out of our own way*, that is, to get away from our negative human aspects long enough to hear what our positive soul has to say, and to allow that soul to direct us. Dr. Wayne Dyer in his book, "Excuses BeGone," writes, *"The new biology says that there's an energy field surrounding, and contained within all of your cells, and this field is influenced by your beliefs."* Imagine then, what could be driving you? With all the trauma attached to divorce, are your cells generating positive energy, or are they beholden to an old belief system and to the many negative emotions (energy) attached to your past and possibly your present? Is your mind controlled by the state your body is in: Stressed out, traumatized, lacking in proper nutrition and sleep, etc?

Luckily, we have options. We can manipulate those cells and re-teach ourselves how to think and change our mind about what we should feel. Dr. Dyer's research led him to believe that our DNA is just a blueprint our body uses to guide us. He writes, *"Your perceptions have the power to change your genetic makeup – your beliefs can and do control your biology!"* This statement helps to validate the manipulation process. Our body can influence our mind, and our mind can drive our body. If we can change our minds by twisting and transforming all negative thoughts and emotions into positive, productive, forward moving feelings and beliefs, then we will have more control over what we say and do. If our souls, not our human selves, help us determine our destination and speak through our navigation system, we will always be led by goodness. Sri Chinmoy's writings teach us, *"We have to offer the mind to the heart. If our focus of concentration is in our heart, then we will easily be able to feel that what is coming to the fore is all sincerity. Inside the heart is the soul. The soul cannot be anything else but a flood of sincerity. More than that, it is a flood of spirituality"*

We keep our sincerity and spirituality by setting goals with altruistic motives attached, and by constantly getting rid of negativity in the vessel that houses that beautiful soul. By purging ourselves of harmful foods and chemicals, polluted atmosphere and surroundings, bad relationships, pessimistic thoughts, emotional traumas and outdated belief systems, we replace negative with positive. Only then can our *will* be considered free. Once we establish what our goals are, our soul energy, the universe, or if you prefer, God, starts to provide the answers to help keep us on the right road. It is our job thereafter to hear and accept what we need to do. As your soul guides you, your human self has to trust the direction it takes you in, which will be to continue to remove all negative behavior from your life and add new, more positive activities no matter how uncomfortable it initially makes you feel. As you do this, you start to see and hear differently, making your navigation system easier to follow. As time goes by, your job to become the best person and parent you can be is easier, more straightforward and uncomplicated.

When we start to change our physical selves (first aspect) and become healthier beings, we instantly change our mental state (second aspect) and begin to think more positively. When we take responsibility for what we put in and do to our bodies, we will act and respond with more love and less anger. When we are not chemically driven by food, drugs, drink and other outside forces, we will see and feel a new truth and not create an unhealthy reality or interpretation of what is happening around us.

We begin to forgive and see the other side more quickly and easily when our moods and emotional state (third aspect) are stable. We learn to live in the present as we begin the long but worthwhile process of clearing out negative emotions and traumas from the past. As all of these first three aspects, the physical, the mental, and the emotional, are being freed from negativity, our fourth and most vital aspect, the spiritual, soulful part of ourselves can come through with even more vigor and consistency.

When we change what is not right (or should I say, not working) within us, our manipulation process will become simpler, with generosity and positive intentions coming faster and faster. In the beginning of this new journey of learning to *Positively Manipulate* energy, it may take a month of Sundays to get yourself to even think a kind thought about your ex, but as time goes on, the easier it becomes, until one day you are just doing it without a struggle. *Positive Manipulation* is a gift we give ourselves and those we interact with. When we are driven by our spiritual aspect, we get what we want, we live blessed and at peace no matter what is going on around us, and best of all, we become the ultimate example for our children to follow.

"I was to the world as insignificant as a speck of sand on the beach, until I became a mother... and then I was someone's universe." – DM

CHAPTER 4
THEY ARE OUR MIRACLES

There is an analogy I use quite often when speaking to divorcing parents: "If your child were sick, you would do almost anything, spend any amount of money, and travel to any part of the world to help them heal. If your son or daughter fell into a well, hundreds of people would gather. One or both of you would be standing front and center with a rope around your waist ready to be lowered down, thousands of dollars would be spent, and the world would stand motionless until your child was safe. So let me ask you, what is the difference now?"

In the event of an ugly divorce, many of us temporarily disregard this standard. While we are in pain, our new focus becomes self-preservation and that generates an entirely different energy. We teach our kids about love and being kind to others, yet we'll spew hateful words at one another. We expect them to share their toys, but we hold back money from their mother or demand property from their father. We want them to love and respect their grandparents, but then we create custody issues and sometimes even worse, cut off all ties with extended family members. We do these atrocities without regard for the emotional health of our children. We the people, the same parents who would die for our kids, use divorce as an excuse to act terribly and wind up mutilating our child's self-esteem and innocence. How does this happen? Is there a decorum switch that is turned off in our parental brains the minute we decide to leave our marriage?

And this is not just an affliction of the non-secular population. I have heard of, and seen personally, couples who are mindfully harassing each other and then going to church on Sunday with the children in tow, trying to hide what is really going on. Perry Netter speaks somberly as a rabbi about his experiences with congregation members: *"Like all clergy, I have seen families hemorrhage as husbands and wives go to war, where every decision is about winning and losing, where the only rule of the game is that the winner is the one who inflicts the most pain. I have sat with mothers who insisted that their ex-husbands could not stand on the bimah with their Bar Mitzvah sons because 'he hasn't been a father to him all these years; he's not going to stand there as his father now.' I have seen parents refuse to walk their daughter down the aisle together on the day of her wedding. I have seen fathers hide their financial assets and cause their children to live in poverty."*

His sad stories are not unlike many that therapists, counselors, attorneys, mediators and coaches like me can retell about our clients, and of our own divorces. At my son's wedding, I was told at the last minute that I would have to walk through the doors of the reception hall by myself and be announced as "the mother of the groom" without "the father" by my side. His excuse for not escorting me was unclear. As my heart broke silently, I held my head up high and smiled graciously in front of 180 people so as not to inflict guilt or sadness on my son and new daughter-in-law. I concur wholeheartedly with Perry when he laments, *"I have seen enormous pain and suffering as a result of divorce. So much pain. And so much of it avoidable."*

THEY WILL ALWAYS BE OUR REASON FOR LIVING WHETHER WE ARE DIVORCED OR NOT

Unless we can empathize with our child's issues and pain, we may not feel we have reason enough to overcome extreme angst toward our ex. Some of my clients have actually asked with intense anger, "Give me one good reason why I would want to stay loving toward her!" Or, "I don't even like him let alone try to love him!" Unless we are altruistic enough to love our former spouse and categorize it as a mitzvah, or a "do unto others" situation, we may need another motive to call on. Wanting to live a life free of anger and pain is not incentive enough for some people, especially those who have been scorned.

We may need to go back to the moment in time we first gazed into the eyes of our newborn and recall the immense outpouring of love we felt. Irrespective of when you first bonded, whether it was right away in the delivery room, or if you are like me, hours or days later, your life changed in that instant and your heart, from that point on, belonged to your child. No one I have ever met has not been ready and willing to die for their kids if need be. I know I would not hesitate to rescue Matt or Heather from a burning building or dive into a shark-filled ocean to save their lives. I would allow a surgeon to cut me open and remove a kidney for my son or a lung for my daughter. Unfortunately, at certain points during my separation, I couldn't even hold my tongue to protect them, let alone give up an organ!

SOBERING STATISTICS

To really help our kids through the divorce process, we need to be committed to doing whatever is necessary to keep them healthy. We need an enormous motive to continuously manipulate our negative emotions, and as far as I am concerned, what better one do we have than the love we carry for our kids? If you need more incentive, here is just a small sample of the statistics I gathered from www.dealwithdivorce.com, proving how devastating divorce can be on children:

- *They are fifty percent more likely to develop health problems than two parent families. (Angel, Worobey, "Single Motherhood and Children's Health")*

- *They are at greater risk to experience injury, asthma, headaches and speech defects than children whose parents have remained married. (Dawson,*

"Family Structure and Children's Health and Well Being" National Health Interview Survey on Child Health, Journal of Marriage and the Family)

- *A study showed that six years after a parental marriage breakup the children tended to be "lonely, unhappy, anxious and insecure." (Wallerstein "The Long-Term Effects of Divorce on Children" Journal of the American Academy of Child and Adolescent Psychiatry 1991)*

- *Teenagers in single-parent families and in blended families are three times more likely to need psychological help within a given year. (Peter Hill Recent Advances in Selected Aspects of Adolescent Development Journal of Child Psychology and Psychiatry 1993)*

- *They are four times more likely to report problems with peers and friends than children whose parents have kept their marriages intact. (Tysse, Burnett, "Moral Dilemmas of Early Adolescents of Divorced and Intact Families. Journal of Early Adolescence 1993)*

- *Children of divorce, particularly boys, tend to be more aggressive toward others than those children whose parents did not divorce. (Emery, "Marriage, Divorce and Children's Adjustment, 1988)*

- *They are roughly two times more likely to drop out of high school than their peers who benefit from living with parents who did not divorce. (McLanahan, Sandefur, "Growing Up With a Single Parent: What Hurts, What Helps" Harvard University Press 1994)*

- *Seventy percent of long-term prison inmates grew up in broken homes. (Horn, Bush, "Fathers, Marriage and Welfare Reform)*

- *They are almost twice as likely to attempt suicide than those who do not come from broken homes. (Velez-Cohen, "Suicidal Behavior and Ideation in a Community Sample of Children" Journal of the American Academy of Child and Adolescent Psychiatry 1988)*

It doesn't have to be this way, but unless we can judge and then curtail our own behavior, can we be convinced that these issues won't affect us and our families? Does this give more credibility to the need to **Positively Manipulate** every word out of our mouths and every move we make? If you are thinking, "This would never be my kids," then I implore you to read on.

ODE TO MY DIVORCING PARENTS

When posed the question, "How are your children handling your break up?" many people grow silent, agonizing over an answer. In fact, when I phoned three divorced fathers to ask if their children would write a letter or poem (for this book) about their families' divorce, two of the men were actually afraid to ask their kids. This makes sense! We decide to marry and create a family, and then later we make the decision to split that family up. It is all within *our* control and the children are left to deal with the repercussions. It is no wonder why we would be afraid to find out how they are handling it. If they weren't "okay" the guilt would be enormous! But it is worth it to ask. Without their perspective, we will never know how to create change.

Simon is an accountant and a very motivated single father. After telling him about this section of the book, he decided to approach his eldest daughter and ask how she was handling their new lifestyle as a divorced family. The next day he phoned me to say, *"Donna I was using your energy last night while speaking to Tracy. I decided to handle it forensically and asked specific questions knowing full well she isn't one to emote. It turned out great and one of the best conversations we ever had. She filled me in on what I was doing right and also what she wanted me to do differently. I was very pleased at the result."*

The Good, The Bad, and The Ugly

The following poems have been collected from children of divorce. They are real, living, breathing examples of what we have done, for better or worse to our children. They have been categorized to re-emphasize how our behavior will influence the outcome of their childhood. While reading, try to imagine being in their shoes, actually living their lives and experiencing a divorce from their childlike stance. Sometimes it is imperative to "get down to their level" to gain perspective and perhaps that is what Abe Lincoln meant when he said, *"We never stand so tall as when we stoop to help a child."*

The Good

This poem was written by my friend Brian's 21-year-old daughter. He decided at the onset of his divorce (she was only one and a half at the time) to do whatever was necessary to assure his children had a smooth transition from childhood to adulthood. No expense was spared; no issues squabbled over. He and his ex-wife worked together to maintain their family unit and here is evidence that their altruistic efforts paid off.

"Our Parents" written by Shannon McMahon at age 21

We may have been divided, torn open at the seam,
But just because they're separate,
It doesn't mean we're not a team.

We may have only had a single parent in our home,
But just because we're different,
It doesn't mean that we're alone.
And just because our parents may not see eye to eye,
They have us in common,
And for our benefit, they try.

Through thick and thin, they give their all
With our best interests at heart,
To create a certain normalcy
Out of the fact that we're apart.

Although they can't both always be the one
To catch us when we fall,
They're both always on our side,
As our parents, through it all.

Shannon describes her home as "single parent" because of their living conditions, but also because her Dad (Brian) was absent much, working many hours to properly support two households. She understood, even as a small child that they weren't really "alone" as she felt the presence of her dad and his love through the way he took care of them. Although Shannon expresses the household may not have been perfect when she says, "through thick and thin", she acknowledges that her parents always worked together with a common goal; namely their children's welfare.

THE BAD

Sometimes there is an inconsistency in the behavior of one parent, perhaps a mental illness, a compulsive disorder, or just an unwillingness to cooperate. The children expressing their emotions in the following writings dealt with much stress during the marriage and the divorce process. Although they survived the turmoil, it remains to be seen how well they handle their own relationships as adults.

"Hurt" written by Ashlea Brunotte at age 15

You left me here all by myself; you went and broke my heart.
By leaving like you did that day, you tore us all apart.

I'm still young and impressionable; I thought that you could see.
The part of me that's reaching out, longing to be free.

You're still my dad, forever more; I know that that is true.
And even though you left my mum, I won't stop loving you.

But my life goes on after you, as your life will also go on.
But neither my hope nor my happiness will undo what you have done.

Ashlea wants to tell her father that she is alone even though she still has her "mum." When she states, "the part that is reaching out, longing to be free" she may be relaying how tough it is to be left behind to hold the family together. When she states her life will go on after he leaves, she follows the statement with, "but neither my hope nor my happiness will undo what you have done." Here she is expressing her doubt that, no matter how good she can make her life, she will never forget or heal from what condition he left her and her family in.

"My Pink Prison" written by my daughter Heather at age 13

These floors have felt too much.
I can still feel them shake.
I'm surprised the tiles haven't shattered,
Along with the red shards of glass stuck to the bottom of my feet.

These walls have heard too much.
I'm surprised they're still standing.
I can still hear them scream.
Even under several layers of yellow paint.

This cold concrete angel has seen too much.
I can still see the fire in her eyes.
I'm surprised she didn't use her wings to hide.
The anger held in her fists left cracks on her stone fingertips.

My tear-stained teddy bear has tasted too much.
I can still wipe water off his floppy ears.
I'm surprised he never choked on my tears,
But I guess he couldn't with his mouth sewn shut.

This little girl has felt, heard, seen, and tasted too much.
I still feel their screaming surfacing my prison floor.
I'm surprised I can even sleep here anymore.
My heart will always be torn between my two heroes.

In this poem, my daughter is describing herself using the marital home to express her sorrow and pain. In the first stanza, she is depicting the floor's instability (*I can still feel them shake*) and explaining how ungrounded it feels to grow up in a divorced household. The second stanza describes the walls, which are her ears that she can't shut off. The cold concrete angel was a statue in front of our house. Here I believe she is talking about her spirit and how from the outside things looked normal, but inside her heart was breaking. In the fourth stanza, her teddy bear depicts her inability to talk or tell anyone how sad she was. Lastly, she tells of her bedroom, which was her sanctuary but often times a prison she couldn't escape. If you notice, she is covering all the aspects of being human; her emotional self (the teddy bear), the mental (walls and floors), her spiritual (the angel) and more obscure, her room or prison, which seems to encapsulate her entire physical being.

"Silent Tears" written by N. John

I sat quietly by my window, as the rain falls outside,
As a single tear slid slowly down my cheeks,
The screaming sound was there again,
Oh those loud screaming, shouting voices.
Another single tear slid slowly down my cheeks,
As I thought, Oh daddy! Oh mummy!
What have I done to cause those loud, screaming voices?

I looked out of the window,
The darkness outside has now become my life.
I thought of happier times when we used to play,
Laugh and talk as one. Oh, how I miss those days.
Another tear slid slowly down my cheeks
As I thought, oh mummy, Oh daddy,
Why has darkness now become my life?
Oh daddy, Oh Mummy
What could I do to make this darkness go way?

Another tear slid slowly down my cheek,
These silent tears are now my life,
Smiling and laughter are foreign to me
Oh mummy! Oh daddy!
The world seems too big for a small person like me
I looked up at the stars and asked the Lord to please,
Take this pain away.

Many children feel responsible for their parent's divorce. In the first stanza, N. John is describing the screaming she hears and is taking the blame for what is transpiring in her life. In the next stanza, she is asking her parents how she can fix the situation or "make this darkness go away." Realizing it may not be all her fault (in the last stanza) when she acknowledges herself as "a small person like me," she is acutely aware of what is out of her control and then asks God for help to resolve the pain.

THE UGLY

Children in this category symbolize the travesty of a truly negative childhood. Their stories are painful to hear, and fortunately, they don't represent the majority, but their perspective is necessary and significant. With their sorrowful words, the next two youngsters poignantly make my point; Irrespective of how much pain a person is in while going through a marital breakup, it can't compare to what a child goes through at the hands of one or both their parents.

"Daddy" written by Veronika J. at age 13

It happened 6 months ago, though it seems like yesterday.
I remember it clearly; it was a cold autumn day.
You told me you loved me then left through the door
Three bags and a suitcase was all you carried,
As you got in your car and drove more and more.
Wet tears ran down my cheek as I heard your last car beep.
I knew the fun times and the games were over,
No more kisses at night no more bear hugs when I'm sober.
No more laughing in front of a warm blazing fire,
No none of that because you're a cold hearted liar.
For 13 years you only cheated and swore.
You weren't the daddy figure I would adore.
You tried your best to be a good dad,
But somehow at the end of the day I would end up being sad.
When I was younger it was easier.
I was put into your arms and you held me tight.
You would never let go if I were scared at night.
But all those moments are just pale memories
Because of you I was left on the bottom of a hole.
I had to find my own way out. It wasn't easy but I survived,
Because my mom and my sister were by my side.
I have just one more thing to say as you live with your new wife,
Just remember you gave a 13-year-old girl life.
And it doesn't matter what you feel or did,
She is still your little kid.

When Veronika describes her father's love for her, she is expressing how easy it was for him when she was small, but as she got older and her needs grew, his love did not. Veronika reminds us that no matter what happened in the past, or what is going on in the present ("as you live with your new wife") we are still responsible for the children that we produced.

"Not Your Little Girl" written by Alex O. at age 14

I was ten years old when a fight one morning
destroyed my family without even a warning.
I was young and dependent and he was strong and wise,
but little did I know my Dad was full of lies.
He made empty promises and he broke my heart.
Through many painful years, my life has fallen apart.
Now he likes to drink to numb his pain away,
while I have to endure intense pain every single day.
I am now 14 years old in this harsh cold world...
If you don't want to be a Dad, then I'm not your little girl.

This poem expresses Alex's deep pain and resentment of her Dad's life-style and choices. She is acutely aware of his inability to father her and decides "I'm not your little girl" so she can sever herself from his behavior. Tragically, she believes that if she can disconnect and not be his child then she will be okay not having a father.

FROM THE MOUTHS OF BABES

Surely when this phrase was coined, the energy behind it was light-hearted and jovial, nothing like what we see here from these creative, yet wounded children. Still, it is the perfect quip to sum up what I am trying to relay; sometimes we have no idea how our children really feel. If you were motivated enough to have read through it, however, you are well on your way to this understanding and have already changed your own energy and the dynamics of your divorce! You have, by now, decided that your children's welfare is more important than any negative emotion you have or can contrive. You are on a journey that can't be stopped, one that will enhance every aspect of your life and that of your binuclear family from this moment on.

As you turn the page on this chapter and move onto Book II, The Ten Commandments, I would like to leave you with one last remark that I hope will work to open your mind and your heart just a smidgeon more. Once again, we hear from Perry Netter: *"If we can focus our energy on our love for our children, we can access that love to help prevent us from hating our ex-spouse and behaving in a way that is destructive. If we can embrace our love for our children and nurture their growth as individuals, we can learn to love that part of our ex-spouse that is a part of our children. If we love our children, we can learn to support that part of our ex-spouse that feeds their souls. If we truly love our children, we won't behave in such a way as to hurt them. And we love our children."*

BOOK II

THE TEN
COMMANDMENTS

*Most of the Commandments have stories attached, but the names and certain circum-
stances have been changed to protect friends, family and clients. Understand that
when I use male or female examples, there is no significance, as I do not blame or
hold responsible one gender more than the other. Herein is an expose of both sides that
should trigger a new reality of fairness to all.*

"By understanding what motivates us to act kindly or with malice, we can begin asking questions about the behavior of others. And with understanding, we can begin loving – not their behavior, but their potential; not their decisions, but their journey. And with love, we can begin healing by example, showing kindness, compassion, and another way."

— Mike Dooley, Excerpted from "Choose Them Wisely; Thoughts Become Things!"

COMMANDMENT I
THOU SHALT NEVER STOP SAYING I LOVE YOU

This commandment is the most profound request I will make of you and it deserves to be the first directive one needs to follow in order to have a healthy divorce. We need to remember, when we make the decision to leave physically, there are still three other aspects to consider: emotional, mental, and spiritual. You are still connected to the person you separated from if you are a parent, and you will be until "death do you part." This is the main ingredient of the marital vows that needs to remain intact. This is the most crucial point in the divorce process: The art of letting go of one aspect while still being able to lovingly hold on to three others.

STARTING THE MENDING PROCESS

When I left my husband, I was determined to make the divorce work even if the marriage didn't. In 1992, there weren't many books written on how to do this. No one was there to instruct me, nor did I know of anyone who had a *good* divorce, so I used the terrible break ups that I was exposed to as an example of what *not* to do. I sincerely felt that it was crazy to love someone enough to say yes to marriage one year, making them the person you ran to with every issue, then turn around some time later and make them into the enemy you were running away from.

Instead of viewing him as my opponent and dwelling on negative emotions that I felt towards his persona and his actions, I decided to achieve the antithesis and encourage the more positive emotions to flow. I wanted to continue to love the father of my children, and I was bound and determined to hold onto what good we did share; namely, the love for our kids. How did I let go and hold on at the same time? Truthfully, I found this easy to do once I realized that I didn't have to stop loving him in order to physically and mentally leave him as a husband. Because of the kind of attraction I still had, getting over him in a physical sense was tough, dealing with the day-to-day issues that arose was mentally challenging, but continuing to love him as the father of my children was natural. It seemed organic, and I never questioned myself about it even when people thought I was nuts, kindly or sometimes rudely pointing out how unhealthy this emotional condition might be to maintain.

To me, it is nutty to ignore goodness so one can concentrate on negative. It is crazy to manipulate love into apathy, dislike or, even worse, hatred. Yes, there is a grieving process and everyone needs to address their negativity about what happened in the past, but those are *our own* issues to deal with and have nothing to do with our former spouse. Once you leave a marriage, you can't keep blaming the ex for how you feel. (Actually you shouldn't have been blaming him/her while you were together, either.)

Even though my ex did things that were cruel, hurtful and egregious to my persona, I was the one who had control over how I felt about it and what I was going to do with my life in the future. The past and its grievances were my challenges to overcome; the present, and how positive I wanted to live my life from that point on were what I was concentrating on; and the future was wide open for everything and anything I wanted it to be. There was no way I wanted to proceed without acknowledging what remnants of good sentiment were still in my memory. I chose to forgive. Quite frankly, I wanted to sew my broken heart back together with soft, pink-colored yarn made out of love, not blood-red sutures of steel wool and barbed wire.

THE ART OF LETTING GO

The process of letting go is not just about acknowledging that you don't want to be with your spouse anymore, it is a four-part staircase with many steps to climb. The four parts are what we have already discussed; namely, the physical, emotional, mental and spiritual aspects that you are comprised of. When we leave the marital home, we *physically* step out, but then we may have to let go chemically and sexually. When we decide we want to divorce or are being told our partner wants to go, we *mentally* have to adjust, but do we ever really examine what went wrong so we can learn and grow, or do we hold on to resentment and pain? Do we accept full responsibility for our actions, past and present, or do we play the blame game? *Emotionally*, we are letting go when we disconnect our caring energy and spousal love, but when we turn it into anger, mistrust, disgust, or any other negative emotion, aren't we still emotionally attached? And when we have children, there is always a spiritual connection because a part of us is living outside of ourselves in the form of human beings we have helped create. If we disconnect *spiritually* from our former spouse, does that automatically disconnect us from a part of those little beings as well?

Alicia,* a spiritual healer and counselor from Brooklyn, New York, gives us an easy to follow, albeit difficult to sometimes achieve, synopsis of how to release one kind of love in order to transform it into another. I so appreciated her writing style and point of view, I asked her permission to share it with you. Use it as a checklist to challenge yourself. Have you accomplished the letting go process in a positive way?

Be Decisive: *If you have made a decision to leave, then leave! If the other person(s) has made that decision then let him/her go! It is to invite more pain and suffering into your life to hold onto something which no longer serves your highest good.*

Face Your Fears: *Fears are created and manifested in the world, by you. Fear of financial ruin, loneliness, safety of your children etc… These fears won't go away just because you chose to stay in a liaison to avoid them. Your fears will be addressed as you confront them. This alone is a good enough reason to let the relationship go. It can bring strength where there was once weakness and fear. Go into your breakup with courage, knowing all endings have beginnings! The trick is to welcome the challenge facing you. See it as an obstacle you can overcome that will make you stronger and then go for it!*

Mourn! *You are human. We are all human and we suffer when we break off relationships. It is within our nature to attach ourselves to others, things, concepts and yet our journey homeward is to let these things go in order for us to grow. So mourn! It is okay, have that good cry. Sometimes it can be so painful that we have to go into escapist behavior; drinking, over/under eating, shopping, Internet surfing, TV-watching etc… to avoid the pain. Be careful for this can be more damaging than helpful. The pain is unavoidable. It's going to happen. The more we hold it in, the more damage it does to us. Let it out! If you can't, then find someone to help you! The more you mourn and clear yourself of the heartache and disappointment, the better you will be in your new life.*

Take Responsibility *for your part in the break-up, even if you believe you are completely innocent. You made the decision to have the relationship for some reason. Own up to that part! For example, if you find yourself in an abusive entanglement, what part of your own karmic energy is contributing to that condition? What part of the self allowed you to stay so long in such unloving conditions? This is crucial, for if you believe you are completely innocent and you haven't done the necessary work of changing and healing yourself, you are bound to encounter the same type of person you are leaving!*

Don't send any negative wishes unto the person. No matter what they have done to you. If she/he is a cheat, liar, etc., by all means call a spade a spade. But don't wish bad things to happen. Why? Because what you send out into the world comes back to you! If you find yourself on the verge of cursing someone, pray to all that is good and holy not to send these negative thoughts. Don't underestimate yourself. The more powerful you are, the more damage you can do and thus the more you can do to yourself. Believe that the Universe is the one empowered to administer justice in a fair and equitable manner. In your darkest moments, rely upon its power.

Forgive! Now you are ready for the final act. Forgive yourself, for having made a mistake, for being stupid, weak, selfish, greedy, unloving to self etc. Send love to yourself. Meditate on it before you go to bed, asking your higher self to heal you. Begin to move away from your addictive behaviors; start to be proactive in your journey towards change and wellness. Love yourself, even if the other person didn't. Don't judge yourself by this failure. For it really isn't a failure at all. It is an occurrence which transpired to help you to become a better person. Become that better person! Don't let this opportunity be wasted on holding onto old ideas about yourself or others. Don't become bitter or revengeful; making promises of never loving again. Begin to think about your new life, the new you and then use love to help you manifest this person. Once you have done this you are ready to forgive others. The circle is now complete — the debt paid! You have mastered the art of letting go!

You will notice that Alicia talks about forgiveness and she starts with, "forgive yourself." This was an important step for me because I felt incredibly stupid, as she puts it, for having brought in such an awful marriage. I kept asking myself, how did I not see it beforehand? Why did I stay so long? Why do all my friends' husbands love and support them without hurting or intimidating them? What is wrong with me that I chose pain? After time, therapy, and a lot of research, I realized, why *not* me! I was the perfect candidate for the kind of behavior that I endured. Having low self-esteem and many emotional and physical (bio-chemical) challenges as a young woman, it made more sense that I would bring in negative behavior from men than it would for me to honor myself by marrying someone that would support and love me unconditionally. After all, I didn't love who I was at all and that was the energy I was enveloped in.

When Alicia says to forgive ourselves for our "mistakes," she is not saying we necessarily made a mistake. It is our interpretation of our actions that counts. When I was young and not aware of how I could change the past by reinterpreting it, I blamed myself for the state of my life. But how could there be blame for not knowing any better? After learning and growing, I realized that I became who I am because of the past and that past was my school; it is what brought me to this point and what gave me my children. I will never regret marrying my ex, most especially when I consider what I got out of it, and that modality and energy is what I use to this day to stay loving toward him.

ALWAYS VALIDATE THEIR EXISTENCE

The best counsel I can give you, the most profound tidbit of advice that is written in this book is the simplest to do: **Never, ever, tell the children that you have stopped loving their other parent!** When it came time to tell my children we were getting a divorce, Matthew was 12 and Heather was about 3. Not that any age is easy, but I believe Matt had it the hardest. Almost a teen, he was in a place of instability and fear. Heather was too young to understand anything more than "You mean Daddy is not coming home?" Matthew had witnessed many fights, much abuse and name-calling. He was severely impacted by both the marriage and the news of the separation.

Driven by a desire to make them feel comfortable, I came up with a scenario to help explain why people get divorced. At that time "Aunt Anita" was living downstairs from us in my two-family house with, let's just say, thin walls. She was always the fun aunt and spent much time with my kids while they were growing up. At the time of my separation, however, she was intolerant of noise and frequently yelled at the kids for making too much of a commotion. Although Matt and Heather enjoyed her immensely, I knew they were sometimes afraid of her moods.

"Okay guys, you know how much you love your aunt right?" They both looked at me with wide eyes and nodded, "Yeah, we love her!"

"Well," I continued, "Even though you love her very much, and she has always loved you, would you want to go downstairs and live with her all the time?" They both instantly shook their heads and Matt groaned, "No! That would be too hard!"

"But you both still love her even though she sometimes yells at you?" Again, more nods, so I persisted. "Then maybe you can understand that Mommy and Daddy love each other very much, but we just can't live together anymore. We adore you and we want to be a family, but not in the same house. What do you think about that?"

Believe it or not, the analogy worked and they seemed to instantly understand the idea of not getting along. Of course, they both spent years in a tumultuous household where fighting, yelling and sleeping on the couch were normal occurrences. Part of their fear of living apart from their father was extinguished, though, just knowing there was still love between us, the love they were created with and the love we still shared as a family. This love energy can transcend all fears and will blanket and soothe a child's aching heart.

At the onset of most divorces, many people sit the kids down and say, "Mommy and Daddy are getting a divorce because we don't love each other anymore, but we still love you!" Guess what? Children at any age, who have absolutely no experience with relationships, have no idea the difference between love for a child and the love between a man and a woman. When they hear this, their existence becomes invalidated and they have nothing concrete to stand on, thinking, "If he stopped loving my mommy, then will he stop loving me?" As far as your child is concerned, "then maybe if I am bad you will divorce me too?"

MANIPULATING NEGATIVE EMOTIONS

Okay, so you have been listening thus far and understand my point but you still can't bring yourself to love your future ex. Here is a reminder: You loved him or her at one time, enough to marry, share body fluids, and co-sign on a bank account. There must be something there you can hold onto in order to keep the next 20 to 40 years of your life from being a minefield of negativity. That is exactly what you are looking forward to if you cannot keep the communication open and the love flowing. Ultimately, the children pay the highest price and if that is the outcome for them, they will continue the tradition and affect every generation to follow. In the words of Gandhi, *"If we are to teach real peace in this world, and if we are to carry on a real war against war, we shall have to begin with the children."*

Take heed of his words. At this juncture, use the powerful energy and love you have for your kids and send out a radar message to your brain to stop and pause at every positive thought you have had about your former spouse. Think about an attribute you admired (there has to be at least one!) or a trait you originally fell in love with. Once you have that thought, create a constructive emotion around it. This is the mental *Positive Manipulation* process at work! Believe it or not, when you do this, you instantly change the energy between the two of you and your ex will now instinctively try to live up to that positive feedback. Mother Teresa had this advice for us. *"Each one has a mission to fulfill, a mission of love. At the hour of death when we come face to face with God, we are going to be judged on love; not on how much we have done, but how much love we have put into our actions."*

FORGIVENESS: THE ULTIMATE USE OF LOVE ENERGY

It may be "forgiving and forgetting" that is precluding you from loving your ex-spouse. Doreen Virtue, in her book "Angel Therapy," put it so beautifully when she wrote the angels' message to us: *"For it is not words that take your hurt away, dearest loved ones, but the emotion of love. You see, love is an ancient electrical impulse that travels along the circuitry within your being. It travels freely and tells its tale of light and laughter. It scrapes away all error residues left along the circuitry as it goes along."*

She writes about love as a means to forgive, but also as a means to take away our own pain and angst about our past. So many of us don't do this, though, believing we need to stay angry in order to be strong. She adds, *"And yet you often short-circuit this gentle messenger for reasons that are still unknown to many among you."* So this begs the question; if we can believe that forgiving someone will help us more than it will help them, then would we choose forgiveness more often?

NEVER MISTAKE KINDNESS FOR WEAKNESS

My old boss used to use this expression all the time, and I'm sure he never knew it, but I felt his words were speaking right to my heart. I look back and realize that in my younger years I covered my vulnerability and pain with a veneer of angry bravado hoping no one would take advantage of what was really underneath. It took a long time to peel away that exterior and go back to being able to expose the side of myself that wanted to be soft, always able to express kindness and love.

From Hinduism, Vidura tells us, *"There is only one defect in forgiving persons and not another; that defect is that people take a forgiving person to be weak. That defect, however, should not be taken into consideration, for forgiveness is a great power. Forgiveness is a virtue of the weak, and an ornament of the strong. Forgiveness subdues (all) in this world; what is there that forgiveness cannot achieve? What can a wicked person do unto him who carries the saber of forgiveness in his hand?"*

So you also know, to forgive does not mean to condone. Instead, we must realize that the energy of forgiveness can help us to overcome all the power that anger, hatred, disgust and sadness can instill. When we forgive, we counteract all negativity and put ourselves on the quickest route of our healing journey. Vidura continues with, *"Righteousness is the one highest good; and forgiveness is the one supreme peace; knowledge is one supreme contentment; and benevolence, one sole happiness".* It is for ourselves and our children that we forgive. The benefactor of our forgiveness may or may not respond, (in human terms, may or may not deserve it!) but that should never be our concern, nor should it preclude us from continually releasing the love energy that allows us to wipe the slate clean.

IF FORGIVENESS IS THE KEY, WHAT IS IT THAT WE ARE TRYING TO UNLOCK?

Dr. Brian Luke Seaward, a noted psychotherapist, says, *"Jesus' message was about love and compassion, both of which follow forgiveness."* I agree with this in some circumstances, but during a divorce, perhaps it is the other way around? If we marry someone because we are in love with them and then they hurt us badly, do we first have to find the love again in order to forgive? I keep meditating on this and still the answer is unclear to me. Perhaps what Dr. Seaward meant is that it is easier to "feel" the love again after you forgive? That I agree with! In any case, challenge yourself to find one or the other and the rest will follow.

I know in my life, it was much easier to forgive family members then friends. Why? Forgiving them is a must in order to keep the family unit in one piece. Even though we choose to love the person that we married and it was not an automatic love like the one we have for a parent, sibling, or child, I believe we should still view it as the same. A family is a family whether it is blood related or not.

On the other hand, many believe it is easier to forgive a friend because you can disconnect from a friend. It is much harder to cut your emotional self off to someone (a former spouse) who is in your face all the time, dropping the kids off, at school functions, or family get-togethers. But this is when it is even more crucial to forgive! Of course, it is a bigger challenge to stay loving when you have a constant reminder of your painful past always present. Understanding that we still need to stay united even though we are living separately is a difficult concept to maintain with problematic emotional challenges, but when there are children to consider, there is no other way to behave. We become permanently fused with the person we marry the minute our sperm and egg merge. It makes us bonded for life, whether we want it that way or not.

NEVER STOP BEING A FAMILY

A really important aspect to maintaining the love in your family unit is to actually go out of your way to keep the family unit. Doing things together whenever possible will promote loving feelings between the two of you and help solidify the children's belief that no matter what, you will always be in it *together*. This is especially true when one parent is emotionally or mentally unstable. Some of us bow out of a relationship happy not to have to deal with an unbalanced spouse anymore, but we forget that our kids are still dealing with that parent, and guess what? Now they are doing it alone without you as a buffer!

A few years after my separation, I met a young woman who was from a divorced family. Her mother was a bit unstable, but her father went out of his way to keep constancy in their lives. She told me how he always arranged for the family to be together during holidays and vacations. Each year they took a trip together as a reminder that they were still united as mother/father/brother/sister. She believed it was extremely generous of her parents to do this, and also said they were the most profound and beautiful memories she had of her childhood.

I took her advice to heart and a year later, when my ex offered, we booked a trip for all of us to visit Disney World. We had never really taken a family vacation together during the marriage except for a few days here and there locally, so this was a true adventure. Luckily, neither one of us was in a relationship so there were no other people to consider. We reserved a two-bedroom suite for five days and the kids had a wonderful time. Of course we made it a point to ensure that they understood the divorce was still permanent. Knowing it could be confusing to them, we concentrated on having fun and creating a loving memory. I am not going to say it was easy for either of us to get along. After all, there were many reasons why we split, and I am sure there are many divorced couples that could not bring themselves to do this, considering it painful or even gut-wrenching. There are special conditions that would preclude many divorced families from vacationing together, and I am not one to promote more anguish.

But if your circumstances allow it, keeping peace for a few days to keep your children stable and happy is a small price to pay. Even if you can only bring yourself to do a one-day outing, the kids will still get an enormous benefit out of it. Matt and Heather's fondest memories of our time together as a family were of spending holidays together. Before their father became involved in a relationship of his own, he would share Thanksgiving dinner with us and often came on Christmas morning to open gifts. This made life so much easier for all of us! Although it was only for a few hours, it was a huge gesture and it meant the world to them.

To keep myself balanced during some of our family gatherings, I would chant to myself, "Chill! You are not married to him anymore." When any annoyance, memory, or potential threat to my esteem occurred, this was a helpful reminder that whatever he did to hurt me before was no longer a factor in my life. The freedom of divorce gave me a certain boldness and inner peace, and that change of attitude generated an energy that could be felt. When an argument ensued, I didn't have the need for self-protection either. The new energy helped me keep my mouth closed from any barking criticism I may have wanted to spew, which helped keep his behavior in check – and the kids definitely benefited from it.

WHEN FORGIVENESS SEEMS LIKE THE IMPOSSIBLE DREAM

After 15 years of marriage, Peter's father became involved with a woman at work. Believing this woman was his soul mate, the father came home one day to announce that he could not decide between staying with his family or leaving and starting anew with her. The decision was made for his father, however, when Peter's mom told him to get out and not return. It was a horrible divorce, painful for all involved, and eventually led to the mother becoming an alcoholic. In an effort to preserve her own feelings, she forbade her former spouse from coming around at any time other then scheduled visitations.

Even though Pete's mother was a deeply religious woman, nothing could console her hurt, and the hatred she felt for her ex-husband was carried throughout all their lives. From graduations to weddings, this man and his new wife were not allowed to participate in any family gatherings or holidays. Peter, not knowing this, would lament, "He never came to school events or even my baseball games."

It was after about 30 years that one of his younger siblings decided "enough was enough" and invited each of her parents to an important family event. Her feeling was, "If my mother doesn't like it, she doesn't have to come!" Surprisingly to all, Mom did attend and as the saying goes, "the sky didn't fall." Although she never admitted to forgiving him, she must have realized how her inflexibility had been splitting the family in two, creating all sorts of dilemmas for them to endure.

This woman's inability to forgive her husband caused pain, remorse, shame and countless other emotions to fester in her children. Half of them sided with their dad and the other half with their mom, causing each one to have their own set of woes to deal with. And the worst of it was that all those years growing up, no one knew the real truth. It was decades after the initial divorce that Peter finally found out the role his mother had played in keeping his father from him. He went through much of his life believing his dad didn't care about him enough to participate in his daily activities. Peter was almost 40 years old when he found out through a family friend that his father did attend most of his baseball games. He was hiding behind the bleachers or distant trees, attending when he could, until it became necessary to move out of state to avoid his ex, her constant tirades and his own pain and guilt.

Although it was satisfying to finally know the truth, this story does not have a happy ending. Peter had to come to grips with what his mother was capable of, and then look at his own life and the course he was on. The damage created by both his parents throughout his childhood made life unbearable and caused all kinds of issues in his adult relationships, leading eventually to his own divorce. Because of the negativity he was exposed to, Peter never learned to forgive. He showed no remorse in the demise of his marriage, blaming his ex for everything, and held onto much anger. Unfortunately, this cycle may continue until he eventually wants to be taught a better way.

TURNING IT ON

Did you know that there is no way to measure darkness? Scientifically, there is only a way to measure light. Did you also know that there is no way to measure cold? There is only a way to measure heat, or shall we say, the presence or absence of heat. If you think about it then, is there no way to measure hatred, just absence of love?

If we turn up a thermostat, there is warmth where there was coldness. Flipping the light switch completes an electrical circuit, generating light where there was darkness. By turning on love and forgiveness, we annihilate anger, resentment, regret, bitterness and so many other negative emotions.

Napoleon Hill suggests this theory when he writes, *"Positive and negative emotions cannot occupy the mind at the same time. One or the other must dominate. It is your responsibility to make sure that positive emotions constitute the dominating influence of your mind."* He calls this process "Autosuggestion" and teaches the "Law of Habit" as a way to achieve it. I call it ***Positive Manipulation***. Again, we are using different words to describe the same process. Either way, it works!

WHEN THEY HAVE DONE YOU WRONG

Many clients will tell me, "But they don't deserve my forgiveness!" To that I answer, "You are not doing it for them. You are doing it for you and your children!" There are often circumstances in a marriage that present a very heavy scale of "blame" to lean to one side. When it comes to abuse, alcoholism, drug abuse, thievery, infidelity and gambling, we would be hard pressed not to accuse one party of more responsibility. Truthfully, this has no bearing on the forgiveness process. It still needs to be done so the party that endured the abuse can be cleansed of negativity.

Sri Chinmoy puts it best in his book, "The Wings of Joy": "*By seeing someone's limitations, we do not help the other person in any way. We only delay our own progress. If we find fault with somebody, his undivine qualities are not going to disappear, nor are ours going to decrease. On the contrary, his undivine qualities will come to the fore in his defense, and our pride, arrogance, and feeling of superiority will also come to the fore. But by seeing the divine in someone, we expedite our progress and help the other person to establish his own life of reality on a divine foundation. We have to see others with the heart of a lover and not with the eye of a critic.*"

To shorten this lesson: When we hold onto negativity, it only hurts us. The other person doesn't win or lose a thing. When we turn on that love switch that exists inside our hearts, however, we rid ourselves of what could be precluding us from having a happy life. The residual effect is also helping the energy between the two of you, and of course, your children. Dr. Karl Menninger says, "*Love cures people. Both the ones who give it and the ones who receive.*"

NO REGRETS

Ever wonder why things got so bad in your marriage in the first place? Certain portions of your relationship had to be okay at one time or you wouldn't have gotten married. Over the years, "stuff" happens, resentments build and the love gets sequestered by it. If you choose to forgive the stuff and drop the resentment, the love comes forth as strong as or even stronger than ever. And it doesn't have to be the same kind of love that husband and wife share. That is not what I am promoting. Now that you are apart, it can be a love that breeds respect and mutual admiration for what you have created together. "Never regret your marriage," I coach my clients. "After all, can you honestly look at your children and believe your time together was never meant to be?"

LOOKING FOR THE GOODNESS

No matter how difficult, *Positively Manipulate* yourself to say, do and feel the most optimistic, always keeping in mind your ultimate goal is to have a successful divorce and parenting partnership, not a miserable broken family unit. In doing so, you can't help but generate positive energy. I remember having such a difficult time in the beginning practicing this "act." Believe me, in the beginning the process may very well be an act on your part. But once you start to look for the positive, you get into a habit that is hard to break. It feels so good to be good, you don't want to stop!

In her book "Excuse Me, Your Life Is Waiting," Lynn Grabhorn writes about her experiences with annihilating negative thoughts, a practice she calls "Tricks for Switching Focus." I love the idea of using trickery, because it mimics the *Positive Manipulation* process and brings to mind what the word manipulation means to most people. Sometimes we do have to trick ourselves into doing what we know will achieve the best outcome. Staying positive isn't easy when your head is filled with negative thoughts, so she helps us by giving easy to follow steps that redirect our focus. Again, no matter what verbiage we use, it is still the same techniques: change your thoughts, they change your emotions, and that changes your energy.

Although with some co-parents it may seem like the impossible dream to think positive about every issue pertaining to our ex, it is worth the effort. When you are divorcing, you have built up a case against your spouse in order to be able to leave. If you were the one who was left, you may want to hate him/her and convince yourself you are lucky to be rid of the relationship. Now I am asking you to persuade yourself that some goodness still exists. Again, use your kids as a motive. Wouldn't it be better to know that your child's mom/dad has good qualities? Isn't it better to believe you didn't make the worst decision of your life by marrying this person? When you start to think this way, it helps you to find the qualities in them that made you want to marry them in the first place.

To get my process started, I began to look at my ex's ability to father. Although I considered him to be remiss in his financial obligations to us as a family, he lovingly adored his kids. He played with them, hugged and kissed them and constantly told them he loved them. My father was a fantastic provider, but never displayed affection for my sisters or me. My heart softened when I realized that I married a man who was capable of this kind of love. I also remember when the kids were quite young how often I would praise their dad for his abilities as a craftsman and carpenter. "Your Daddy can build and fix anything. He could have been an aeronautical engineer!" After some time, it was easier to find qualities I admired. After all, it wasn't that long ago that I pledged, standing in front of an altar and two hundred friends and family members, to honor him. The least I could do was keep that promise.

FINDING THE REASON TO THE QUESTION, "WHY?"

When it comes to unbearable emotions, *Positive Manipulation* is our only recourse. We need to shift our perception from *the ruination of a marriage* to the realization that *divorce is the start of a new life*. Believing that this is our lesson to be learned makes the process so much more palatable. Once we do this, it is easier to shift our view of the person we were married to. I live my life by this creed. As I recently told my client Sidney, "Consider yourself a bolt and she (his future ex-wife) is your nut – pun, in this case, definitely intended! You fit each other perfectly and were brought together for a unique and special purpose. Learn the reason and lesson for your union, and all that you have lived through starts to make sense. No matter how painful it seems now or how horribly it may end, your time together becomes worthwhile." He said, "You mean there is a reason why I got screwed?" I laughed and said, "Sorry for such a blatant analogy, but yes, nuts and bolts can only come together one way."

As Dee Wallace puts it in her book "Conscious Creation": "*We have all been taught that the world happens to us, and that we are not the cause of our world. So how can we own our consistency? Most of us are locked in victim consciousness whether we acknowledge verbally, emotionally or vibrationally that life happens to us. We put it off onto luck; we put it off onto God, fate, bad timing, I just fell in with the wrong people, or my body's supposed to be this way.*" What she means by this is that we attract every incident we live through in our lives. Remember when I said we should take responsibility for everything that happens to us? When we do this, we actually change the outcome from something that could be perceived as disastrous to something worthwhile to help create change. In Dee's words, "*If everything happens to us for a reason, the people and circumstances we are allowing to block us are actually gifts, if we choose to shift our perceptions. So forgiveness is another tool we can use to keep us from remaining stuck in our lives. It allows us to move into a higher vibration.*"

THE TENTH STEP

Many people can understand the concept of learning from mistakes, but when asked to take it to the next level and actually find forgiveness for someone who hurt us, the forgiveness becomes an enormous and continuous challenge. While writing this book, a coaching client, Tom D., offered this advice to my readers:

> *Dear Donna,*
>
> *In AA, which may be viewed as a spiritual program, we work the Twelve Steps to recovery. While I was in the middle of the legal portion of my divorce, which took about four or five months, I would read Step 10, which, among other things advised me that through "courtesy, kindness,*

justice and love" it would be possible to come into harmony with practically anyone.

By practicing "courtesy, kindness, justice and love" to the best of my ability, what could have become a very acrimonious process became fairly peaceful and quiet. In fact, the relationship now, while not filled with an abundance of joy, is one of mutual respect and care.

Best regards, Tom

No matter what your reason for holding onto negativity, I implore you to think about the repercussions to yourself and your children. In a world that exists with so much destruction and sorrow, shouldn't we be doing anything we can to shield ourselves and our family from more negativity? Keeping hatred from our hearts will keep our inner realm peaceful and harmonious. In the words of Sri Chinmoy, *"Only two miracles are worth seeing: The miracle of loving and the miracle of forgiving."*

"There were three of us in this marriage, so it was a bit crowded."

Princess Diana

COMMANDMENT II
THOU SHALT REMAIN LOYAL TO THY FORMER UNION

PLEASE DON'T MAKE YOUR SEPARATION INTO A THREESOME

Commandment II has been expressed by many experts as a warning, but most separating couples refuse to listen. Here it is again, though, coming from a different perspective: Two minus one equals one, not three. **Don't bring another person into your equation!** Besides the confusion and upheaval it causes the kids, divorce is hard enough on us as adults, and doing it while we are trying to have a second relationship is almost impossible. I know many people who have tried and the success rate is so incredibly low, we have to ask ourselves, "Why would we even bother?" Unfortunately, many of us feel we cannot be alone or go through the pain of leaving one person without having another one waiting in the wings. My ultimate advice (which comes from intimate experience on the subject) is stay alone until the paperwork is signed and then for some time after, for your sake, the kids and any unsuspecting person you may attract.

TIME FOR HEALING

I used to joke about the condition my life was in after my separation by saying, "I'm not fit for human companionship!" And I was right. Before, during your separation and for some time after the divorce, you cannot send out the right signals to attract a healthy relationship with someone else. The person you seek may be great, beautiful and ready, but you are not. This could ruin any chance for a future with them.

Unfortunately, we are chemical beings. Some scientists believe we have what they call a "feedback loop" that may keep us in a holding pattern with another person. Almost like a drug, even a bad relationship can create a physical addiction that can alter our bodies right down to the cellular level. By bringing in another person, we can break that feedback loop with the introduction of his or her biochemistry. It is the equivalent to using methadone to get off heroin. Unfortunately, if we don't take the time to learn about ourselves and heal, we could be going from one bad drug to another!

Besides the bio concern, there are so many emotional and ethical issues to consider. If you are a single person and thinking about dating a separated person, then run, run, run as fast as you can. You can't catch him if he's a married man (or woman). And if you are separated, please don't pull anyone into your mess or you will be hurting one more innocent person who will be expecting more from you than you are capable of giving.

MY STORY

Six years after my separation and divorce, I met a married man through business. For him, it was love at first sight, or so he thought. It turned out to be lust at first sight and an escape from his sexless marriage. After trying for months to get a date with me (to no avail), I finally put my foot down and demanded he stop. With as much bravado as I could muster, I lashed out, "I don't date married men! I don't care if you have a terrible marriage and are one foot out the door, unless you are single, have your own place and divorce papers; I will not go out with you!"

A few weeks later he told his wife he was leaving her, had an apartment rented, and paperwork started with his attorney. He showed up at my door on a new motorcycle (I am a sucker for a Harley guy) and I finally conceded to dating him when he moved into his apartment. Looking back, I believe I felt sorry for him. He seemed so miserable, and I had just had my heart broken by another man the year prior. I thought he was sweet and genuine and would never hurt me. Oh boy was I wrong! As a life coach, I should have known better, but my need to heal him and my desire to be in a loving relationship won out. Even though I knew he would be torn, I disregarded my gut instincts and became involved with him, which led to a serious relationship. Unfortunately, his wife didn't know about me, (first sign of a disaster) and when she found out, there was hell to pay and much guilt on his part. I say this all the time to clients: "You need to get out of a marriage with the exact same love, dignity, and grace that you went into it with. No compromising and no exceptions!" So why didn't I listen to my own advice?

During the entire relationship, I kept breaking up with him, demanding he not return unless he was divorced. He came back to me, time and again, sometimes begging while promising the paperwork was in the process/filed/ signed or whatever story of the moment. I trusted his earnest attempts – I am sure he meant it at the time – but the agony dragged on for just under three years. At a certain point, I believe I was only going back with him each time to prove we were soul mates and destined to be together. That, of course, would justify all the trouble I was causing by being the other woman. Nevertheless, there was no justification. I went against my own hard and fast rule and got what I deserved: low self-esteem, an empty, broken heart, and a new life lesson I will never forget.

In the end, I felt sad for his wife, and even though she was well taken care of financially, I had tremendous guilt over being part of the demise of their marriage. Obviously, if it took him almost two and a half years to get an uncontested divorce with no kids involved (they were already grown and belonged to her) and no money issues to resolve (he gave her everything) there must have been love there. I came to the conclusion that I was his toy, but she would forever hold the title of *wife*.

After waiting so long for his divorce, the day finally came and a short time later, we became engaged. I think it was just two months after I got the ring that I gave it back (actually I returned it to the store and had them send him the check), knowing the marriage would never work. So much damage was done, so many lies told and so much hurt caused that it was impossible to believe we were meant to be together.

However, this story has a twist. It was about two years later that an e-mail came into my box. It was from the hosting company that held the domain name for the website I helped create for this man's company three years prior. I called his office to give him the info and guess who answered the phone? You're right; his former wife! She had much to say to me, as you can imagine, but mostly wanted to tell me they were married once again and living a wonderful life together.

It was probably a shock to her when I exclaimed with a tearful cry, "I'm so happy for you!" The news was just what I needed to hear to heal my shallow opinion of myself. Although self-forgiveness should be a part of our everyday lives, I didn't think I could ever let go of the thought that I ruined a marriage. Realizing she wasn't dealing with a wretched home wrecker, she graciously told me that their marriage was in disarray when I met him and she understood why he wanted to leave. She also said their relationship had never been better and gave his affair with me partial credit for creating their new and improved bond.

HAVE THE COURAGE TO LEAVE FIRST

Even though I am taking responsibility for my participation in this love triangle, he was responsible for what he did to his family. He wasn't strong enough to be true to her or himself by getting out of his marriage first before entering into another relationship. Not only did he tear apart his own family, he jeopardized mine as well. Convincing my mother, sister, and children of how much he loved me, put everyone in a moral dilemma. Overall, he was acting selfishly by following his human weaknesses and only thinking about what he wanted, which is a very dangerous state of mind when you are part of a family. If he had listened to his soul from the beginning and not his aching loins, he would have heard the message quite clear. Instead, he acted on what his body wanted, and then listened to his soul later, which came out in the form of guilt, a useless emotion once the crime is committed.

DAN AND CARRIE

Some believe the person they have just met and are willing to leave their current marriage for is *The One*. That could be, but if you don't leave your first marriage before you start your new relationship, you may not have the right to expect blessings during your lifetime with this new person. The Law of Return applies here; whatever you create and send out in the form of energy, you will eventually get back.

Dan and Carrie met at work and started out as friends. Both were in what seemed to be good marriages, or so that is what each of their spouses thought. Dan was very unhappy living with what he considered to be a domineering wife, and Carrie felt suffocated and sequestered living with her parochial husband. The two spent a couple of years as co-workers before they decided to have an affair. As fate would have its way, they were caught first time out by Dan's wife. The repercussions that followed couldn't have been more disastrous. They were forced out of their homes, alienated from their children and almost lost their jobs. So you know, these two were incredibly good individuals who never meant to hurt anyone. Both were very religious and this single act in no way should define them as human beings. However, their love for each other and their desire to be together took precedence over any practical behavior, and the results were devastating.

It wasn't long after the separation that Dan's future ex-wife became despondent and tried to commit suicide. His children, who were the most perfect, well-mannered kids you could meet, became unruly and for a short time unapproachable. Thankfully, Carrie's family stayed strong, but her parents and siblings wouldn't speak to her for quite some time. Even though their lives were falling apart around them, the two were deeply in love and after spending much time with them for some years, I have to say, they were true twin souls.

They planned to marry just as soon as their divorces were finalized, but their bliss was short-lived when Dan was diagnosed with terminal cancer. They chose to marry anyway, and for the next several years, they spent countless hours, even weeks at a time in hospitals, opting for intricate surgeries and drastic treatments to keep him alive and stable as long as possible. Luckily, all their children and family members forgave the two their indiscretions, making these years extremely healing, emotionally if not physically.

To his credit, Dan broke all kinds of records in the field of medicine and stayed on Earth as long as he could to be by Carrie's side. Their love and bond was truly miraculous and beautiful to watch. During his last months, he and I reminisced from his hospital bed about our friendship before and during his marriage to his first wife. Knowing through years of research that negative emotions stay stored in our bodies and play a role in our physical well being, I dared to ask him if he felt his divorce had anything to do with his illness. "Could it be," I asked softly, "That you never really got over what happened to the family as a result of your affair?" He tilted his head towards me and gazed with eyes that were almost void of life. "I don't know," he muttered. "But I wish to God I had done it differently."

I always told my kids, "There are really very few bad people in the world, just lots of good people who sometimes do bad things." The problem is when you are a good person who is doing bad for any reason, legitimate or otherwise, it will carry a devastating effect that can last forever. I would never blame Dan's cancer on his desire to cheat on his wife. Instead, I believe he couldn't *resist* the disease because of the guilt he carried with him. He was such a wonderful, spiritual man and I don't suppose he ever really believed he deserved happiness after his actions hurt so many people.

IT TOOK TIME TO GET IN. IT TAKES TIME TO GET OUT.

Divorce is never really taken lightly, but most people are led through their lives by a societal rule that says, "Everyone deserves happiness." The key to this rule, however, is not to *take* your happiness at the expense of others. There is always a graceful and unselfish way to achieve your goals. Take the time to get to know yourself again. Allow your children time to heal and to get used to the idea of sharing you with someone else.

PAUL'S STORY

Paul came to my home office one day complaining that his children did not respect him. Filled with an indignant attitude of "I give them everything!" he was completely ignorant of the fact that he devastated their lives just a few years prior by having an affair with a younger woman that caused the demise of his marriage. Fortunately, he decided to break up with the woman to go through his divorce alone. He spent time healing his wounds so he could become a better father. It was only two years later, though, that he became lonely and even though he wasn't sure he could have a lasting relationship with her, he decided to bring his ex-lover back into his life. He expected the children to respond with tolerance and respect, but instead they became angry and pulled away from him. By the time he came to me, they were spending all holidays and living full time with their mother and didn't want much to do with him.

What Paul did not consider was how the children would feel being around the woman that broke up their family. Although his son was a tiny bit sympathetic and showed some appreciation for his needs, his daughter was furious, considering how this affair affected their mother and the family. Paul was only considering his own feelings without regard to everyone involved, including his girlfriend. He put his kids and his ex through an emotional wringer for years and as soon as they began to feel somewhat comfortable with their situation, he brought the pain right back in. The worst part of this is he didn't get it at all.

There wasn't much I could do for him at that stage except point out that his children's lack of respect was based on his lack of discretion. If he loved this other woman (who was about 18 years his junior, making things even more difficult) and wanted to create a life with her, he needed to be ready for the impact it would create. Looking back, he realized it may have been better to keep his relationship with her a secret from his children until he knew it was going to become permanent. Instead, he just expected them to deal with another hurtful decision that he felt he needed to make.

OUT OF THE MOUTHS OF BABES ... AGAIN

Not wanting a revolving door of men for my children to deal with during my divorce, I never allowed the kids to meet anyone I dated. Actually, I wouldn't even consider a man I went out with to be a "boyfriend" for fear that my ex would get wind of it and the children would be affected by his angst. So I stayed single for five years until I believed I met "the one." Henry was a great guy and a great dad. I thought I had hit the jackpot and soon after we met, we were talking marriage. Because he had a child my daughter's age, we often did fun things together and quickly became a little family. Unfortunately, my daughter never dealt with my relationship with him, nor was he able to handle her. On many occasions she was absolutely insolent, and would not allow us to even give each other a peck on the cheek without causing a stir.

When asked why she acted this way, Heather's answer was, "Mom, he is a liar and I don't trust him!" This coming from a nine-year-old seemed incredible, and I am not sure to this day if she was being psychic in deciphering his energy or just acting spoiled, but she was right. Confused and in enormous pain caused by his own divorce, he wound up hurting us terribly and it took years for me to recover from the breakup. In fact, it was one year after this relationship ended that I decided to have the affair with the "semi-married" man. One would have to deduce that my actions were partially driven by the pain I was still in from the breakup with Henry.

The point of this story is that I am not sure when it is a good time to bring another person into *your* life after *your* divorce. Only you and your family will know and it should come after careful consideration, a lot of therapy, family discussion and soul-searching. Whether you wait months or years, there is always a risk to your family unit, your self-esteem and your children's welfare. I do know that nothing has to be rushed, and unless you are completely sure you will marry this person or that they will at least become a permanent entity in your life, do your kids need to be worried about or involved in your adult relationships?

CONSIDERING THE EMOTIONAL STATE OF YOUR FORMER SPOUSE

Sometimes it is even more important to ask, "Can my ex handle it?" I always thought I wanted my children's father to be the first to marry. Knowing how he might handle the news if I was the first, I deemed it easier to be the one to take the emotional hit. I knew I would help my kids to see the positive side of having a new family, and I always vowed to show my best self irrespective of the pain I might feel. As fate would have it, he did become engaged first and lucky for all of us, she was a wonderful woman I believed would make a great step-mom. It was barely a challenge to make the transition.

Unfortunately, this is not always the case. We, as parents, must always think twice, then three times, before we involve our children in our love lives. Have your kids sit with a therapist or counselor to ascertain whether they can emotionally handle it. This might feel like the ultimate sacrifice, but look at it this way: If they can't handle it, your new relationship will be incredibly difficult to maintain, and starting out that way, can hurt or even cripple your future together.

THE BEST RELATIONSHIPS COME FROM FRIENDSHIPS

I know, it is so cliché' but it is true! We all hear stories about couples who were friends for years before they became lovers and decided to marry. I have heard it said to me, "I hated his personality when I first met him, but as I got to know him and what he had to offer, I fell in love." It takes time to get to know someone, but we unfortunately believe that love is based on a physical attraction that most of us call chemistry. If that comes first, friendship is sometimes difficult to achieve, and there is also the nut and bolt theory to consider. Is this person another lesson to learn from? If you didn't learn from the first one, guaranteed, you will bring in another relationship that will fit perfectly into your lesson plan.

If you meet someone and become friends first, you will always know it is based on real love and compatibility and not lust. Pay homage to your family unit by remaining single until you are actually single – emotionally, mentally, spiritually and *legally*. If you meet your soul mate during your separation period, (or when you are married) know that if it is real, it will last and it will be better if you do wait. In a real love situation, Father Time is on your side and could never get between the two of you. Remember that.

"Make the most of yourself, for that is all there is of you."

Ralph Waldo Emerson

Commandment III
Thou Shalt Love and Take Care of Thy Self

Commandment III is for the body and soul, but it reflects plenty on how we handle ourselves and are perceived by everyone around us, most especially our kids. Children of divorce are having enough trouble keeping their own life together, let alone needing to help a weak parent. By maintaining our health and instilling wellness into our daily lives, we remain strong and stable, allowing for a positive perspective of our new life conditions.

This Commandment encompasses "all there is of you" and therefore needs to be stressed fervently. I will repeat this statement throughout the book because it is so crucial: Without a clean, strong, positively energized body, you can never achieve a clear head or a forgiving heart. The strategies listed in this chapter are being offered by an experienced coach, but more importantly, a divorcee just like you! Remember, I had no prior skills or coping mechanisms going into my divorce. Instead, I gleaned what I could from reading, seminars, research and trial and error, taking advantage of what came naturally to me and more importantly, what was free. This is the most important chapter you will read!

PUTTING YOUR BEST FACE FORWARD

We need to make it our job to stand erect, put on our best face and smile whenever we can so the kids believe everything will be all right. It is important to know that they don't understand the concept of time. You may realize that there is a mourning period, but they may not grasp it before feeling the effects of your anxiety or depression. It is imperative that both parents appear brave and in control of their lives. After all, if you don't, what sturdy leg do the kids have to stand on, or if you want a male perspective, my friend Richard proposes, "What strong shoulders do they have to lean on?"

So shave your legs, ladies, and guys iron your shirt. Both of you put on your most excellent outfit, and style your hair, even if you can't bring yourself to care. You still have to face the world and your family and yourself in the mirror every day. If it is loneliness that is dragging you down, remember always that even if this relationship didn't work and someone has left you or you left them, you are not destined to feel alone or be alone forever if you don't want to be. When the time is right, there will be love again if you desire it.

If you are the one leaving because of situations beyond or within your control (you are leaving an emotionally unhealthy person or had an affair), guilt may make it hard to care for yourself right now. Instead, my message is to pay more attention than ever to your own body and it will reflect in how well you handle each stage of your divorce, including communication through body language. When you feel good about yourself, you project a certain bravado that translates into how you take control and handle situations. Also, watch what foods make you feel depressed or moody – it will help you to manage anger, fear and anxiety. Taking care of your body will pay you back with an increased level of self-esteem and control just when you need it most, and more importantly, the children need to see you coping (and eventually thriving). Always remember how you look from their perspective.

The Food/Mood Connection

To thine own self be true... Is this possible? To be true to yourself and show who you really are at every moment seems almost impossible when you consider that we are basically a bunch of chemicals, cells and enzymes tucked under skin. At any given moment we can react to any number of biological changes from outside (and inside) sources. Many people don't understand the correlation between what we put in (food chemistry) and what comes out (moods). During times of stress, we eat lots more comfort foods, like chips, pasta and desserts. The biochemistry that eating these carbohydrates creates in your system could make it very difficult to handle the challenges of this dramatic and often traumatic time. Food and its chemistry can make you feel tired, cranky, anxiety ridden, even angry; and in my professional opinion should be considered one of the highest forms of *negative manipulation* you can do to your body. My daughter and I know this first hand, as we are very sensitive to everything we ingest. Just eating dried cranberries or drinking cranberry juice, which is loaded with sugar, can make us feel ill tempered and, as we put it, "wanting to bite people!" Too much chicken and the aspartic acid it produces in the body triggers aggressive behavior and anger spurts. For about 24 hours after eating simple sugars like candy both of us feel so much dread and doom we could cry for hours.

Feelings Aren't Right or Wrong, but are They Real?

During times of stress, reality (what is really going on here?) is what we should be striving for. During my years of coaching, I have seen many marriages in disarray because one partner or both are drinking and eating harmful foods that change each person's perspective and personality. Case in point: Steve complains that his wife is constantly on his case about every little issue and he has no idea what mood to expect from her when he comes home from work. She blames him for all of her woes and refuses to listen to reason.

After spending time with Steve's wife, Anna, I find her to be potentially menopausal, overweight, anxiety ridden, angry at the world, and looking for the reasons why she is so miserable. After examining her diet and obtaining blood work from her doctor, we came to the conclusion that she is diabetic addicted to bread and pasta, someone who craves and eats candy regularly, has all the symptoms of Candida*, and is hormonally imbalanced. With all of these issues to contend with, Anna could never look at her life realistically. She was so far gone by the time I got to her that she wasn't capable of taking responsibility for her own feelings and was instead, trapped by her body's negative state. Needless to say, this couple was heading for divorce, and in the mindset she was in, it wouldn't be an easy one. Whether she was with him or not, she would still be blaming him for everything.

As part of his coaching, I asked Steve to contemplate a truism I wrote years prior: "If the eyes are the window to your soul, then know that the mouth is the door to your persona. Whatever you put in (food) will reflect in what comes out (negative or positive verbiage)." In other words, Anna became a victim of biochemistry and less than who she really was. Spewing her negative thoughts and emotions daily, her entire demeanor changed, and if we didn't modify the biochemistry creating this persona, Steve would never be dealing with the real Anna.

Throughout the years, I have seen all sorts of food habits that cause terrible addictions, even drinks as apparently innocent as diet iced tea contain enough chemicals (namely aspartame and other artificial sweeteners) to drive people to do and say nasty things. Remember: **Without a clean body, one can never have a clear mind**! It is our duty as loving people to continuously look at our own participation in our life and not blame others for how we feel, think, or react.

Instead, we need to incorporate the *Positive Manipulation* philosophy each and every time something bothers us and ask ourselves, "Is this emotion or mood I am in right now based on the current situation or am I reacting to something that is going on in my body? Is it a hurt from the past?

Is this my reality or is it contrived? What did I eat or not eat that could be causing this mood?"

My daughter and I actually ask these questions to ourselves when we feel out of control, especially sad, or anxiety ridden. Sometimes we remind each other, "Did you eat in the last few hours? (Not eating can cause just as much angst, instigating low blood sugar and dehydration.) If the answer is yes, we ask, "Well, what did you eat that could have triggered this response?" We are both extremely aware of how our emotions can be swayed by our minds and worse, how our minds can be swayed by our bodies, potentially building up a huge case against even the most innocent circumstances.

We choose how we go forth and what attitude we take, but if we are driven by a negative body, we will never know the truth and reality of what is really happening in our lives. In my assessment, if we were eating properly and not negatively manipulating our bodies with terrible food chemistry, many marriages would be saved, or at the very least, many divorces would go more smoothly. By taking responsibility for how we feel and deciding if that feeling is based on reality or not, we will have better relationships going forward.

WHAT TO EAT OR NOT TO EAT

Unfortunately, there is no easy way to find out what your food intolerances are. The elimination diet (which can be found on the Internet and in the library) is the only way to really determine what might be affecting you or a loved one. In books to come I will be giving more guidance about the biochemistry in each food and what it can trigger in the human body, but in the meantime, stick to what I call "clean foods," meaning anything made by God and not man. Some people call this the Jesus diet. Eat all the Omegas you can get in by adding fats like avocados, raw nuts, salmon, organic-cold-pressed (raw) extra-virgin olive and coconut oil to your diet. These foods are crucial to keeping moods in check and depression at bay. Take supplements from companies that promote chemical-free, no-additive formulas. I use liquid (sublingual) vitamins and herbs (lots of B complex and D 3) because they are more readily absorbed. Buy organically raised poultry, including eggs, and whenever possible, eat raw foods.

Despite what most people believe, it is not more expensive to eat well. Real food satisfies us so we eat less, which means we spend less. It doesn't have to be time consuming to eat healthy either. In fact, once you start, you will notice how much more energy you have gained, physically and emotionally. Your mental acuity changes, which will make you more productive minute to minute, and you will find stress easier to handle. So much so, that once you start, you will never stop wanting to do more and more good for your children's health and your own. Each party benefits, by the way, because a person who is feeling this good, spreads the goodness, and that means everyone is a winner.

BREATHE!

Seems to be such a simple task, but few of us take in more than 10% of the oxygen our lungs can handle. Most especially during times of upset, our bodies automatically want to contract, constrict and contort in order to get through an episode. It is my opinion that every time we do this, we help the body store the trauma we are experiencing and that comes out later in the form of more emotional stress. It is so easy to remedy this, although not many of us think to do it. Just breathe, and when you do so, the body can't contract so easily! Try it and see. Take in a deep breath and attempt to make a muscle in your arm at the same time. You really have to think about it. Imagine doing deep breathing exercises during a quarrel? How much arguing can be circumvented if we were all going around inhaling and exhaling? Sounds too easy, right? It is a well-known fact that Zen monks use breathing in their meditation process. By bringing in more oxygen to the brain and other parts of the body, we come to a more relaxed state. Once in that state, we can see more clearly, hear more succinctly and manage our emotions better. Again, some advice from my friend Richard, who says when he needs to get himself out of a stressful state, he repeats a mantra:

"Breathe in well being. Breathe out resistance." By thinking these statements while actually doing the deep breathing exercise he is engaging in a ***Positive Manipulation*** process, which immediately changes his thought process and the energy around him. He took this tip from watching tapes by Ester (Abraham) Hicks who acknowledges, "Deep breathing increases our vibrational connection with source."

The way others perceive us will change as well. Have you ever witnessed how cats behave when they become afraid or angry? They puff up to appear bigger than they are, hair standing on end, teeth and claws exposed. Believe it or not, we as humans do the same thing. I used to watch my husband's eyes go from blue to black, his veins would pierce through his neck and his fists clenched every time he became enraged. This was his response to stress and anger. When I saw it coming, I would become like the cat, and take my position in battle. This was a protective device, although it never really worked because it made his mood worse. When you practice breathing techniques during times of duress, you will change your appearance and that alone can change the energy between yourself and another. It will take you out of a tense, hostile modality and into a more gracious, accepting one.

"BEND OVER BACKWARDS" DURING YOUR DIVORCE

I write continuously on my websites about yoga, and for good reason. When outside stress enters our lives, we often times feel helpless or hopeless. Yoga puts us back in tune with our strengths and lets us know we are capable of changing our existing status. Many people tell me, "I can't do yoga. I am too inflexible." To that I say, "All the more reason why you should be doing it!" In fact, the only inflexibility that could keep you from doing yoga is your inflexible belief that you can't do it! In case you think you are too old, EVERYONE at any age can do this exercise. Yoga can enhance balance, maintain or create flexibility and strength in your spine, joints and muscles, and increase concentration no matter how young or old you are. It brings your body back in time to a child-like state of flexibility, agility and endurance. In fact, I got over my fear of aging the first time I put my foot behind my head in yoga class and naively said to myself, "Wow, if I'm this good after only practicing for one year, I can't wait to see how great I'll be when I'm 90!"

Many athletes who weight train, run or cycle, believe their muscles are too inflexible to do yoga. I tell them, "on the contrary!" Everyone can do it because yoga is the practice of bringing **more** flexibility to your body no matter what state you are in. If you were Gumby, yoga would be redundant! Instead the more inflexible you are, the better your practice can become and the more results you will experience. I like to tell the story of my neighbor, Bobby Nystrom, who is a famous hockey player on Long Island from the 1980s. When I met him, he was into ice climbing, iron-man triathlons and other extreme sports, leaving him in incredible physical shape. Although he was interested in taking yoga, he believed he was too stiff. "I can barely bend," he told me. "Great!" I responded, "If you are stiff because you are muscular, it means you are strong." Even though brawny muscles have a hard time bending, I told him not to consider stiffness to be a weakness, but instead, "add yoga as another dimension to your exercise routine enabling you to become even more powerful. Yoga can take that strong muscle and teach it to be flexible. For an athlete, that's a combination that can't be beat!" One month later, he and 10 of his friend were doing yoga with me, and I have been using his name ever since to entice other athletic men into joining my Sunday morning "Stiff Man's" yoga class. It is such a joy to watch otherwise tight muscled guys get into splits and straddles. Some say it is their favorite workout all week.

On the opposite end of the spectrum are people who are stiff because of injury, arthritis, age, weight or just lack of exercise. Yoga is the absolute best way to ease into any exercise routine! Most other forms, most especially sports, come with a certain amount of injury risk. Yoga, however, can support an injury-free transition into a more active lifestyle. Although I originally started my yoga practice for research purposes, I was totally hooked when I saw the way it was sculpting my body, and as a divorced woman in her 40s, it also healed me of my fears about aging. I can remember vividly having bad days in my 20s, waking up, looking in the bathroom mirror and saying to myself, "I had a rough night. I'll look better tomorrow." Then in my 30's, the "ugh, what happened here" look was blamed on diet and lack of exercise, but still I believed I would look better the next morning. In my early 40s, however, I woke up, looked in the mirror and the realization came: "It isn't going to get any better, is it?"

Most likely, the fact that I was left for a younger woman at the age of 39 (by my ex-boyfriend Henry) prompted my need to achieve the best body I could. It wasn't long after we broke up that I considered plastic surgery, bought every video I could find on the Pilates fitness system and started to buy anti-aging face cream by the bucket load. Since the onset of my yoga practice, however, I have never felt better. I wake up every morning with such alacrity; go to the mirror to check out what new body changes have taken place and smile. Yoga reverses the aging process to such a degree, you actually can't wait to see what more yoga and more time doing yoga can do for you.

And in my experience, the physical demands of the practice combined with Pilates were entirely noticeable within just a couple of months. Muscles I didn't even know I had started to appear. (One day I thought I found a hard lump in my arm until I noticed it was also on the other side. Turns out it was my triceps! Who knew?) Weight came off easily and I noticed less lower back pain, greater endurance and, thanks to the breathing techniques, my complexion got clearer. All this and much more.

GOING BEYOND YOUR DISCOMFORT LEVELS

Another incredible facet of exercise in general, but most especially yoga, is that it teaches you to go beyond your level of discomfort in order to reach a goal. After a while in my practice, I noticed that pain didn't hold me back any longer. If I felt severe tearing, trust me, I wouldn't have moved forward, but I began to recognize hurting associated with danger to my body and hurting that was really just fear based. A sore, tight muscle or Charley horse held me back in the beginning, but as my yoga training continued, I was constantly challenging myself to let go with each breath, ignoring the little aches and pains in an effort to go further and further into each pose. Of course, this translated into the breaking of habits and old belief systems in the rest of my mental, emotional and spiritual life. How could it not? But it was the challenge to my physical self that triggered all this growth.

How Does Exercise Enhance Our Emotional Aspect?

Obviously, the positive physical changes in one's frame will elevate self-esteem and help promote better body image in all age groups, but because of the endorphins released in our body during exercise (especially the breathing techniques taught during the yoga practice), there are even more profound occurrences. A serenity-like condition is produced between your body and mind. This tranquil state relieves tension, which **takes away anxiety**. It helps you go beyond any perceived physical limitation which enables you to **conquer fear**. The hormones produced will alter your mood and outlook helping **release anger**, vengeance, guilt and other negative emotions.

How Does Exercise Facilitate a Healthier Mental Aspect?

Yoga, walking, running, cycling, tennis, swimming, dancing; whatever form of movement you choose, will help to eliminate blocks caused by physical or emotional traumas. Anxiety, pain, fear, or any negative emotion can actually constrict our breathing, making it harder to deliver oxygen that helps us make neural connections. Deep breathing done during all exercise rejuvenates and oxygenates your cells faster and helps to distribute them throughout your body including your brain. These physical aspects facilitate a more positive mental outlook. It's hard to be depressed when you feel so rejuvenated and filled with endorphins. The mental benefits are always different for everyone, but none of us can walk away from yoga,

Pilates, Step, or cycling class without a clearer picture in our mind of what positive attitude we want to continue with for the rest of the day.

Another great mental feature is the practice of visualization. During a yoga class, the Yogi will talk their students into a pose. If someone can't quite get into the full posture, he'll ask them to "picture" themselves there, meaning to take their body as far as it can go physically and then use the mind to take them the rest of the way. When you do this consistently over time, your body finally listens, and you eventually get into the full posture. Conversely, if you never picture yourself in it, there is usually no potential to ever get the full pose. Essentially, when your mind starts believing, "I'm going to let my body go further today," it does. I found this fascinating and decided to challenge myself, taking on the process as if it were an experiment in *Positive Manipulation*; using your mind to push your body beyond where it *thinks* its limits are. Time after time the method proved itself and eventually affected more than my physical life. As milestones were reached, my way of thinking about myself began to change, and I no longer believed in the concept of limitations. Instead, what I couldn't do at this moment became just another doubt to circumvent and a challenge to overcome, and it was just a matter of time before I would be able to do everything I "set my mind to do." My body finally convinced my mind that I was invincible… Or was it the other way around?

HOW DOES YOGA AND EXERCISE ENHANCE OUR SPIRITUAL ASPECT?

Although I have been writing about spirituality throughout this book, it is such a catchall word. Perhaps, though, we can all agree on one facet: It is the practice of bringing oneself to a higher form of consciousness or, otherwise put, the belief that we can connect with a higher power within ourselves and/or the universe. I can tell you with all honesty that exercise has enhanced my soulfulness, and it has brought me closer to goodness, but it is not my religion or form of worship. My beliefs about God were always there and they have not changed because I sit in lotus or stand on my head a few times a week. What has changed, however, is my ability to quiet my mind and to bring more spirituality into my life at any given time. I have acquired more wisdom about myself, and have less desire to hold onto negative thoughts, feelings, or emotions, which allows me to feel closer to what I aspire to be.

Although all forms of exercise are worthwhile to explore, there is none that holds more prominence in my life than yoga, because of the ability it has to prompt such peacefulness. If it was the language my body used to converse with my mind, somewhere along the line, my mind decided there was no better way to live, and that is why I am using up pages of this book to bring it to you. I thank the Hindus for creating this practice and for all the entities over the centuries that have kept it alive. After all, something that is over 5,000 years old and still going strong must be admired and deemed extraordinary. As I tell my students, "Yoga is the only form of exercise that gives your body the flexibility of a 9-year-old kid, and at the same time allows your mind to receive the wisdom of a 99-year-old prophet." What more could you ask to get out of one hour a day?

LISTENING NEVER "FELT" SO GOOD

When I first became separated, I would lay Heather down to sleep at about 9 p.m. and put Matthew – a teenager at the time – in charge of looking after her. With my aunt living downstairs, I could easily slip out and head down to the beach for a long walk. I am not sure if it was the combination of being by the water and the exercise that was so healing, or maybe the music playing in my headset, but many nights I would just cry from relief and happiness. The tears came easily as I acknowledged how privileged I was to be free of pain, and continuously amazed at how incredible it felt to just "be." An aria playing in my ears as the smell of salt air was tickling my nose – how many people can be happy with so little? But truthfully, was it so little? Fact was, I had finally escaped from what I considered to be a harmful marriage after years of trying. I was healthy enough to be able to work hard and earn the money to buy my own home, and just blocks from the beach no less! I was strong enough to overcome my fears, and I was humble enough to understand just how much the universe was helping me.

I knew it was a special gift to be able to enjoy nature and its offerings, but more importantly, there was an intrinsic understanding of how the simple things I did for myself were having the most profound effect, music being one of them. Jacques Weisel, in his book, "Bloom Where You're Planted," says it so perfectly when he writes, *"Music transcends race, religion and national boundaries. It sweetens a sour mood, it makes the body move, it takes the mind off one's troubles as the alpha waves flow. Music blocks our pain and inspires the imagination. Music is power and powerful music stimulates."*

As it soothed my nerves, readying my body and mind for its next set of adventures, I was grateful to use it as a resource during my divorce process. Over the many years since, I have been using different compositions to enhance or change my moods, from Indian drums that help synapse neural connections and inspire me to write, to New Age and its smooth style that melts away my anxiety. It is no joke when they say "music calms the savage beast," but perhaps people don't really understand the true meaning of that quote. It may very well be the negative *human* beast within each of us that settles down as notes play in our ear.

Not all songs work for all people. As I walk, I sometimes need motivation to keep going, in which case dance music works best, although opera holds its special place as well. When I need inspiration, I play albums like "Sacred Earth Drums" (which supposedly mend an aching heart) or instrumentals from the Andes such as "El Condor Pasa," which help me write prolifically. Tim Janis, who is a truly gifted and inspired composer, can immediately stop any negative mood I am in. Recently, my friend Janine turned me on to Jim Brickman, another great artist whose music encourages stillness.

Music can bring you out of the darkness and into the light. It is a like a present we give to ourselves, and it should be an integral part of everyone's healing process. Many lyrics and melodies are written by talented writers who are tapping into aspects of themselves that most of us don't even know we have. That is why particular songs can transcend language or traditions; they connect people to that part of themselves that is yearning for expression and release. And the best part is that it is inexpensive, sometimes free, and can be shared.

DANCING BRINGS FAMILIES TOGETHER

When I was a little girl, my dad introduced me to Tommy James and the Shondells, the Four Seasons, the Beach Boys, and many other artists from that era. We would have so much fun down in our finished basement dancing for hours to rock and roll. My mother wanted no part of it. A product of the 50s (but probably a throwback to the 40s), she only had ears for swing, big band and some mild bop tunes, but she never stopped us from enjoying ourselves and sweating up a storm.

When my kids were growing up, they also listened to that same genre, along with opera and disco. Both Matt and Heather enjoy all types of music and, in fact, my daughter absolutely loves Frankie Valle to this day. When we saw the Broadway musical "Jersey Boys," we couldn't help but get up in the aisle to dance. When it brings people together, music creates a shared energy that can keep you motivated far longer than working out without it. Being an avid exerciser, many people would ask my secret to having so much endurance. These individuals would confess how difficult it was for them to exercise, but I would notice that if you got those same people to a wedding and played the oldies they love, they would move and shake for hours! Music keeps you going and gives you endurance. It seems to transcend aches and pains while it puts you in physical harmony with your body.

When I coach families, I always introduce yoga and dance. Most often, the kids show their parents the newest hip hop moves and the parents get to make fools of themselves impersonating John Travolta in "Saturday Night Fever." Although my kids still laugh at my dancing to this day, (I tell them, "You should be so lucky to have moves like me!") it is another fun way to make us feel connected as a family.

I know it seems trivial, but please, don't ever underestimate music's power to heal and soothe your body and mind's woes! Between the physical aspect of dance as an exercise, the mental aspect of making neural connections and the emotional aspect of calming your anxiety, music is a complete package everyone should take advantage of. And I haven't even mentioned the spiritual benefits! When was the last time you heard a song that made you cry in gratitude? If you are lucky, you hear one every day.

THERE IS A REASON WHY WE SING WHEN WE WORSHIP

Just recently I attended the inauguration of a friend[*] of mine. Being installed in public office and representing a very diversely ethnic county, he decided to have as many representatives of the community as possible attending. There were spiritual leaders from every religion and people of every race. At the end of the service, the minister of a Gospel Church gave a short sermon to congratulate the new officeholder and then introduced the church's choir to sing. Suddenly, from the back of the room, an entourage of at least 30 people came marching in, single file through the doors, clapping and singing "Put a Little Love in Your Heart".

As they came down the aisle, the entire audience enthusiastically started singing with them, and as we all clapped and swayed to the music, tears came rolling down my cheeks. I couldn't help it. The incredible energy of the room generated by hundreds of people singing in unison about, of all things, my most important message, LOVE, was just too much to hold back. It reminds me once again that there is an inherent physical/spiritual motivation for worship using song. It is as if our souls are using music to cut loose of the bodies that confine them so they can remind us, "we are here, and we want to be heard."

---

[*]   Edward Mangano, Nassau County Executive

MEDITATION

When I was about 30, I was introduced to meditation at a spiritual retreat I attended. The weekend was designed to help us learn new ways to connect with God and meditation exercises were offered. Even the mere thought of lying still petrified me, but I gave it a shot and after trying to settle down in a group setting, I wound up running from the room in a panic. Since that incident and for some years later, I wouldn't even consider doing it again, or for that matter yoga, because I was so afraid of the thought of lying motionless trying to empty my head. Turns out, what I was really afraid of was what images would come in when I did finally turn off my mind. Having such terrible memories from past traumas locked inside, part of me was absolutely dead set against unleashing them. No, meditation did not seem like a good idea.

As you already know, I did end up taking yoga (only because my first teacher promised I could leave class before the meditation began), but it bothered me that I was allowing fear to stop me from experiencing what everyone else thought was a wonderful form of relaxation. One day, I was pondering these fears while gardening. When I asked for a solution, a thought came to me as if it was being whispered in my ear, "Prayer is when we talk to God. Meditation is when we listen." What a profound notion! I knew instinctively that this wasn't my thought though, so I ran inside to write it down, wondering who or where it might have come from.

A few days later while watching television, I became riveted to a news show that was reporting on the Guinness Book of World Records. I had no idea at the time why I was so spellbound by the women with the longest fingernails, or the girl with the tiniest waist, but I kept watching anyway with total fascination. At the end of the segment, they reported on a man who called himself Ashrita. Ashrita held the record for the most world records, if you can believe that. He did unusual things like rolling an orange across the floor for one mile using his nose, or juggling while hanging upside down from monkey bars. "This guy is a kook!" I thought to myself, "but I love him!"

At the end of the show, Ashrita was asked how he obtained his skills and concentration. He attributed it to a meditation process that he learned from a spiritual leader named Sri Chinmoy. I was startled (although I should know better) that I had just asked the universe to show me a way to overcome my fear of meditation and learn to lie still without panic, and here was an answer coming in on my TV! Knowing without a doubt that I was being shown *the way*, I immediately Googled Ahsrita's name and found his website. I wrote to him and hoped for a response.

Two weeks went by and I never received an email. I figured if he held 60 world records, he must be a busy guy, so I decided to Google Sri Chinmoy instead. As I perused Sri Chinmoy's website, I was amazed at his teachings and incredibly prolific writing. I was also surprised to find out he had just died, and saw that people like Nelson Mandela and Bill Clinton attended services in his honor and were admirers of his work. Curious about his meditation and eager to learn more, I clicked on one of his writings and saw 12 words that changed my life forever: "Prayer is when we talk to God. Meditation is when we listen."

I always believed that most of what I compose comes from a higher source. Carl Jung called this the "collective unconscious." I never thought I had the IQ to come up with some of the concepts that find their way into my head. Often times, when I "hear" something, I don't even understand it for many months. Instead, I give credit to myself for being open to hearing what wisdom is out there and then sharing it. I put pen to paper and allow for a stream of words to flow. Some people refer to it as "automatic writing." It wasn't until that day though, when I saw the words of Sri Chinmoy in print, did I have proof of what was happening to me. And it gave me one other tremendous realization that I was looking for; just because I wasn't lying still or sitting in lotus position, didn't mean I wasn't meditating! I was doing what is called moving meditation, which is when your body is in motion, but your mind is not following. Instead it drifts and sort of lets loose, becoming empty long enough to receive messages. Ever drive somewhere and then when you arrive, not remember how you did it? Same deal, and I had been doing this type of meditation for years while gardening, driving, walking, showering, doing the dishes – and the list goes on.

Although it is absolutely a legitimate form of meditation, I still wanted to learn the traditional method. Ashrita did eventually get in touch and was happy to lead me to classes given by Sri Chinmoy's followers in Queens, New York. Can I admit to you that even after taking the course, I still don't like to sit still and empty my head? But that is okay. I use it instead to *listen,* which makes me feel like I am still *doing* something. I am of the belief that all forms of meditation are worthwhile, including guided sessions done by CD or a live speaker, moving, transcendental, Vipassana (using the breath), silent, staring at candlelight, and mindful done while breathing. I have also used meditation tapes created by a company named Centerpointe. They apply subliminal messages embedded in intricate musical compositions to help you get into an "alpha/beta" state of consciousness.

Candace Pert tells us, *"Meditation is just another way of entering the body's internal conversations, consciously intervening in its biochemical interactions."* I so believe this, and have come to find it amazingly healing for all four (the physical, emotional, mental, spiritual) human aspects. That is why so many major medical establishments, like the Mayo Clinic and National Institute of Health, are doing experiments with guided meditation and showing miraculous results healing disease. The January 2011 issue of "Consumer Report on Health" states, *"Meditation induces rapid physiological changes, including reduced blood pressure, heart rate and muscle tension. It might also reduce cardiovascular risk, ease depression, and help people with chronic pain, fibromyalgia, headaches, irritable bowel syndrome, multiple sclerosis, psoriasis and Type 1 diabetes."* The lesson here is that we can generate all kinds of negative activity in our body, even on a cellular level, by just living an ordinary life, but through meditation, we can actually be led back to health and wellness no matter what shape we have gotten ourselves into.

When we choose to use the ***Positive Manipulation*** process, there is a continuous need to transport ourselves to a higher awareness, and meditation is the most effective way to get there. Remember, we don't have to know how to manifest what we want. We just have to want it and the ways to make it happen will come to us. Clearing our head and asking for the wisdom to come in accomplishes this quickly and effectively. All great minds will admit to being able to bring in messages from a higher source or part of themselves. When I spoke in a previous chapter about being guided by our soul (navigation), I was intimating this very process. Napoleon Hill wrote, *"The great artists, writers, musicians, and poets become great because they acquire the habit of relying upon the "still small voice" which speaks from within, through the faculty of creative imagination. It is a fact well known to people who have 'keen' imaginations that their best ideas come through so-called 'hunches.'"* What he is saying is that we don't necessarily have to start out being visionaries, or imaginative people. This sounds like an oxymoron, but we just have to be *open* to *closing* our own human mind so our soulful energy can connect us to infinite wisdom. Carl Jung would have us believe it is our primary job as humans. He said, *"Man's task is to become conscious of the contents that press upwards from the unconscious… As far as we can discern, the sole purpose of human existence is to kindle a light in the darkness of mere being."* If this is true, it is not just our responsibility, but more like our life mission to stay in tune with what messages are trying to come through.

"A mother is a person who seeing there are only four pieces of pie for five people, promptly announces she never did care for pie."

Tenneva Jordon

COMMANDMENT IV
THOU SHALT SHARE ALL THY WORLDLY GOODS

Commandment IV helps to keep you in balance with your surroundings. Don't squabble over possessions. Give every marital asset you are supposed to give to your soon-to-be ex with the notion that in the future you will get back everything you need.

Mitch Albom retells a story told by The Reb in his book, "Have A Little Faith": *"That reminds me of something our sages taught. When a baby comes into the world, its hands are clenched, right? Like this?" He made a fist. "Why? Because a baby, not knowing any better, wants to grab everything, to say, "The whole world is mine." But when an old person dies, how does he do so? With his hands open. Why? Because he has learned the lesson." "What lesson?" asks Mitch. The Reb stretched open his empty fingers. "We can take nothing with us."*

AN EASY WAY TO SHOW LOVE

One has to wonder, if we come into the world with no possessions and we leave with no possessions, why do we hold on to so much in between? As soon as my ex found an apartment, I started separating the assets. My goal was to make the transition simple and easy, no squabbling, and no difficult decisions to make. The motive behind it was for the kids once again. I thought if they saw their dad in a tiny apartment with no furniture and homey effects, they would be miserable and guilt-ridden.

He was opting for a studio apartment, but at my urging, he rented a two-bedroom so the kids would have their own sleeping quarters. I brought over all kinds of home goods, including furniture, curtains, towels, kitchen supplies, toys, pictures and the like. I even helped decorate the place, and made photo albums for him to keep around, ensuring a woman's touch and a feeling of home. Let me say, this wasn't as easy as I make it sound. My first instinct was to hold onto to every spoon, knife, plastic cup, and trinket, but I knew it would benefit all of us if I went beyond fair. Believe it or not, how your ex lives reflects on you as a person, most especially to your children. If there is a disparity between households and one parent's living quarters seem desolate, the children may feel guilty for having more, they may not want to visit, feeling uncomfortable in the surroundings, and they may even resent the parent who is living well. Of course, there can't always be an exact split and many parents prefer the children live in the marital home with their surroundings in place so as not to disrupt their lives, but we have to keep in mind that if both parents aren't at least comfortable, the kids will feel it and be affected by it.

FAMILIARITY BRINGS COMFORT

My advice to all divorcing couples is to set up both your places using some marital furniture so the kids can feel familiarity in each space. Sometimes, one parent would rather buy all new. If you can afford it, go ahead! But at least keep some toys and knick knacks from the family home, most especially group pictures and albums. My ex and I displayed family pictures in both our residences during the years the children were growing up. He pinned old photos on his refrigerator and I kept an array throughout the house and in the kid's rooms, all reminiscent of good times we shared.

Although it is sometimes very difficult and painful to look at your former spouse and yourself in a cozy family shot, it is imperative for the kids to believe they are still part of a family unit. It is also important for them to trust they came from love and are still living in love.

If you have been left with nothing and are starting from scratch with little money, don't despair. A home is created by the energy of the people in it, not the box they are surrounded by. Paint new colors in each room and gradually buy some furniture even if it is from St. Vincent De Paul or the Salvation Army. Check with your friends and relatives for hand-me-downs, and make spray paint your medium of choice. During most of my marriage, I had very little money to spend on household items, so it was easy when it came time to decorate my new residence. Used to doing things on a budget, I became a garage sale queen! I salvaged and restored lamps, tables, desks; you name it. One of my favorite corners of the house was one I created with a pressboard table that had a cloth thrown on top (I still have it to this day). I filled it with pictures and bric-a-brac. The house always looked snug and warm, no matter how little I spent on it.

When You Can't Keep the House

When it comes time to sell a marital home, many parents feel extreme guilt for the kids. Although it is true that moving is stressful and sometimes traumatic, it is worse for either parent to feel pressure caused by lack of money. This is the kind of energy that transcends and is difficult to suppress. It is important to make the kids feel comfortable, but it is more important not to go into debt to stay in a house. That is far worse of a strain on everyone! Instead, understand you can create a home anywhere, including an apartment. The children will eventually feel good about their surroundings if you feel good. It is all in the perception and energy you create. Again, a great story from Mitch Albom's book, "Have A Little Faith" that will help shed light on how little an impression a house address leaves on a child's mind:

A soldier's little girl, whose father was being moved to a distant post, was sitting at the airport among her family's meager belongings. The girl was asleep. She leaned against the packs and duffel bags. A lady came by, stopped, and patted her on the head. "Poor child," she said. "You haven't got a home." The child looked up in surprise. "But we do have a home," she said. "We just don't have a house to put it in."

A Little Extra Cash Can Go a Long Way

When our house was sold, I thought my son would never forgive me. Needing to go to a different school, he hemmed, hawed and wallowed in self-pity for months. No matter how much I told him we would be better off, he resisted the change. Eventually he came to realize how easy life became without a huge mortgage for his mom to worry about. I will never forget the first time the kids and I took a trip to K-Mart after moving to the new neighborhood. It was late and we were rushing through the aisles looking for what we needed to buy when Matt turned to me hesitantly and said, "Hey Mom, can, um, can I get some socks?" My response was almost immediate, and as I opened my mouth to form the word "NO", I stopped to think for a second. Realizing that I had some extra cash for the first time in many years, I allowed a new word to roll off my tongue. "Yeah. Go ahead!" I blurted out, "and while you're at it, get some new underwear, too!"

The kids and I were used to having no money and always struggling to pay a mortgage and get out of debt. From having our electricity turned off and running out of heating fuel on a monthly basis, to eating jelly sandwiches and boxed macaroni and cheese when it went on sale, four-for-a-dollar, lack of money was an issue during my marriage. It was unfortunate, but I was constantly saying no to their requests. This time, I realized I had a few extra bucks to spend on what they needed and wanted. It was such an incredible feeling to be able to say yes and to see his face light up at the prospect of having new tube socks!

WHEN DAD AND MOM FEEL COMFORTABLE, SO DO THE KIDS!

Dan, a client of mine, told me of the conversation he and his 19-year-old daughter had about the first apartment he rented by the shore. "We were reminiscing about the great times we had on their visitation weekends. After my divorce, I wanted to keep the kids in their own house, but all I could afford was a tiny one-bedroom for me to live in." Dan's face lit up as he described his little abode. "You wouldn't believe the view I got to look at every day, or the miraculous meals I cooked on a 20-inch stove! The kids were only 4 and 8 at the time, but we have only wonderful memories of our experiences there. The rooms were so small the bed took up all the space, so we used to play board games sitting Indian style on it. We had so much fun in that apartment!"

After hearing the enthusiasm in his voice, I couldn't resist offering my opinion. "Could it be that being by the water made you comfortable, helping you to heal, and that in turn helped the kids?" "Yes," he said emphatically. "In fact, I had our parish priest visit me and after seeing the surrounding water he remarked at what a healing place it was. He reminded me that I get to constantly look at 'all that God has done.' Even though it was so tiny, I loved it and it was the best place to be for me and my children."

FENG SHUI IS YOUR BEST FRIEND RIGHT NOW

You may not realize it, but there are "things" existing in your home that may be causing negative energy to flow. If you hold onto possessions, which also represents holding onto the past, you may never let go of your issues with the divorce. Most people fight for the household stuff, but when you stop to think about the negativity it generates when you know the other person wanted it or needed it more than you, or worse, when good or bad memories instigate pain in the present, it just makes sense to rid yourself of it. Feng Shui, which means wind and water in Chinese, is an ancient philosophy of design. It is the belief that all objects contain energy, negative or positive, and can generate a feeling of peace or unease, depending on different variables. By ridding your home of negative articles, you can start to bring in new, positive ones, which generate a healing energy you could never achieve surrounded by constant reminders of the past. It is an enormous contribution to your healing process.

When I began my Feng Shui practice, I asked my mentor what to do first. She said, "You must get rid of everything that holds negative energy." I started to wonder how I would know, but before I could ask how, she mysteriously quipped, "You will know." She was right, and as I began to rid my quarters of broken items and knick-knacks that held bad vibrations, I realized just how negative my household was. It was a pleasure to keep purging those terrible memories. Out went plants that were half-dead, the old stemware I got as a wedding gift from my pessimistic grandparents and the favorite statue I glued together after it was thrown against a wall. All were constant reminders of what I wasn't willing to forget. They were also a sign of what I may not have wanted to forgive. Some were offered to my ex or made it to the trash; others were fixed and donated to the Salvation Army or given to a needy friend. After the process was finished, I felt light as air and ready to establish my new life.

GETTING STARTED WITH THE CLEARING PROCESS

To begin this process, you only need desire, time, and a garbage pail. Hold each item in question in your hand and ask yourself, "Does this feel good or does this bring in a feeling of discomfort?" Most of the time, you will get an immediate internal response. If not, put it aside for the time being and keep going. When I first took on the challenge of cleansing my house, I was hesitant to toss my possessions away. I am not a pack rat, but even bad memories are sometimes difficult to throw out. Somehow we believe they (negative memories) give us strength and some kind of bravado, protecting us from being vulnerable in the future. Truth is, the items you are holding onto may actually be making you weaker, especially if your ex wants them. Keeping or throwing out an item of worth, even if it is only of sentimental value to your ex and carries no dollar value, will definitely generate negative energy for you. Is it worth it? No! Hand it over, no matter how angry or bitter you may initially feel.

JACK AND JILL

One day right before the holidays, Jill came home to find her entire apartment dismantled. In an angry rage, her husband Jack had left, taking with him as many marital possessions as he could fit in his rental truck. Hysterical and devastated, Jill called me to help and I immediately ran to her aid. When I got to the apartment, she was crying, her eyes swollen and red and the place a mess. Of course, he took all of his property, but marital furniture was also missing, and a valuable painting that belonged to her was taken down from the wall. Even Christmas decorations were gone. Truthfully, I have helped many families clear, redesign and reorganize their homes, but I had never been in this kind of situation before. My instincts took over and I began to hurriedly Feng Shui each room. Filling in the voids by rearranging the remaining furniture, then adding decorative flourishes with what bric-a-brac was left, I made it homey enough to stop her sobbing. I was not sure what was worse at that point, the condition her home was in or the fact that he left her without warning. Turns out that his leave-taking was really a relief, but the finality of it, typified by the emptiness of her living quarters, was enough to throw her over the edge. There was a certain cruelty to how he decided to end their marriage and that realization hit her the minute she walked in the door on that fateful day. One of the most difficult aspects of a nasty divorce is in the awareness that someone who loved us so much before could be capable of such cruelty later.

When it came time to actually get divorce papers signed, Jill asked for her painting back, since she had bought it before the marriage and it was worth over a thousand dollars. Jack refused and a year later, the two were still not divorced because of that artwork. Is there a right and a wrong here? Does it even make sense? Either way, Jack will receive the worst end of this deal. If he wins, he has to look at that painting every day of his life, and in the back of his mind will be another picture of the beautiful wife he left in the middle of the night. Unless he is heartless, that should grate on him forever. Although he may feel justified now, one day it will catch up with him. Negative energy always does.

CREATING NEW MENTAL REMINDERS

After living through a divorce and then some really painful break ups thereafter, I can honestly say, the Feng Shui process offered tremendous healing, while at the same time giving me power to forge ahead on my own. Getting rid of the old, painting, renewing and refurbishing was more than just a form of decorating. It was as if my body was a personified version of my house. What I couldn't change about my circumstances, my emotional or mental state, I could change about my surroundings. Feng Shui offers us an opportunity to gain power and work on areas of ourselves that might be too tender in the beginning of a divorce process. By the same token, take care not to go too far. Sometimes, moving too much energy too quickly can create issues as well.

JACOB'S STORY

After helping my client Jacob condense the contents of his former marital home into his bachelor pad, I knew there would be repercussions. Not wanting to get rid of the expensive furniture he shared with his ex-wife, I reluctantly helped him redecorate his entire house, trying to squeeze every item we could into his current space. Within weeks of doing so, he met a woman, immediately fell in "love," and then moved her in after dating only two months. It wasn't long before he realized he had made a mistake and moved too quickly, but unfortunately, there wasn't much he could do. After uprooting her from her home out of state, he felt guilty and couldn't bring himself to ask her to leave. I was devastated because I knew I had a part in his uneasiness, knowing full well he would feel tremendous loneliness being surrounded by all his marital possessions with its memories and energy attached. The worst part of it was that the new girlfriend was surrounded by all of this, including his ex-wife's energy and mine, because

I was the one who placed every piece of furniture, area rug and knick-knack! Imagine the trouble she must have had trying to adjust to her new surroundings.

During the entire process, I warned him that the movement of energy may be too quick and powerful, but truthfully, he had no real options. Still, this big, strong, macho guy doubted that something emitting from inanimate objects could cause any issue. Ultimately, Feng Shui is about positive change, but it can be overwhelming. In some instances, you may feel too much movement and need to slow down the process. No matter how fast or slow you move though, being in charge of your destiny and enhancing your surroundings is the definitive goal. Eventually, my client broke up with his transitional woman and settled into his home alone. We both learned valuable lessons and I will never go against my instincts again. My suggestions: By being aware of energy shifts, you can eliminate some of the stress. Seek the advice of an expert if you have to, or read about your options in the many books offered on the subject. It doesn't ever have to be negative if it is done right.

WHO SAYS YOU CAN'T TAKE IT ALL WITH YOU WHEN YOU GO?

Sharing doesn't mean deprivation for one, it intimates an equal distribution between two, but many people act as if giving up half their assets is like handing over their left ventricle. The reality is stuff is just stuff and can be replaced. Peace of mind and heart is priceless. We can't feel at ease in our own lives if we create dis-ease in another's. We might not be able to take everything with us when we leave a divorce, or the Earth for that matter, but, if we choose to, we can walk away with what we hopefully have earned to date; namely, honor, dignity, integrity and grace. Gandhi told us, *"Kindness trumps greed: it asks for sharing. Kindness trumps fear: it calls forth gratefulness and love. Kindness trumps even stupidity, for with sharing and love, one learns."* In the spirit of kindness and fairness, we must rest in the knowledge that when we do right by others, whatever is supposed to be ours in this world will come, sooner or a little later.

"I hate to be a failure. I hate and regret the failure of my marriages. I would gladly give all my millions for just one lasting marital success."

J. Paul Getty

COMMANDMENT V
THOU SHALT NOT MAKE MONEY THE ROOT OF ALL ISSUES

Commandment V is perfectly segued by IV: **Don't withhold money from your ex-spouse!** This goes out to men and women who are paying late, not paying at all or who feel their spouse doesn't deserve it. Granted, there are some unfair settlements out there and many people feel they have been monetarily shafted, but most custodial parents with full-time responsibilities deserve ample compensation.

WHAT'S FAIR IS FAIR

Money is just green paper, but we give it so much power. It may or may not be the root of all evil in our society, but it is definitely the root of most evil in a divorce. In a perfect world, we would sit at a coffee table, discuss who makes what, how much is needed and what each person's earning potential is, divvy it up and call it a day. Instead, we fight, argue and waste time, money and energy trying to keep what may not necessarily be ours. I have to ask this question: By not giving what you are supposed to give, what do you really get to keep? More importantly, what do you really gain?

I used to tell single fathers that complained about paying support of my own experiences as a struggling single mom. Because I had full-time custody, I had very little opportunity to earn more money on the side. A person without custody has their own set of woes, but often he/she can come and go more easily, take any kind of job and often, have fewer – and sometimes no – responsibilities for the children's sick time, days off from school, summer vacation or religious instruction. This, along with household expenses, is worth way more than normal child support rates.

If you are a man or a woman withholding money, think about what it is doing to the other person, the children and their life style. Comfort level at this time is of prime importance. A grieving divorcee, especially one who is raising your children, doesn't have the energy to be constantly worried about finances and that kind of negativity directly affects the kids. Help them, yourself and the kids by handing it over if you have it, and if you don't, find a way to earn it. And speaking of earning, are you one of those folks that is not seeking employment so you can do better in your settlement battle? If you are taking more money than you need (most especially if you are not working so you can get more support) what example are you setting for your children? Eventually, you are going to need to carry your own load. Doesn't it make sense to start your new life with independence and self respect, obliged to no one but yourself?

HOLDING HER HEAD UP HIGH

My mom and her sister grew up in a divorced family. My grandfather barely took care of them financially and my Nana lived with constant fear she wouldn't have money to pay bills or feed her children. I will always remember the story my mom told me of not having a nickel to pay for a newspaper, so she stole one from the local grocery store, hoping to help her mother look for a job. They ate potato soup as a staple, and since there was never any money for a babysitter, my mom and her little sister would sit on the porch after school and wait hours for Nana to come home from work.

You would never know they were poor though, because Nana made the best of her situation. While they sorely needed it, she never went after my grandfather for money. Unskilled, she took a job in the garment district as a button-holer and provided what she could for her household. My mom and her sister always looked clean and neat with crisply starched blouses tucked into beautifully hand-sewn skirts. They were well nourished and lived in Brooklyn, in a tiny one-bedroom apartment where they shared a queen-sized bed and sofa to sleep on. It didn't matter that it was small though, because Nana fixed it up beautifully, and years later when my mom and aunt left to be married and have children of their own, all of us grand-children were ecstatic to visit what we called "the dollhouse".

Irrespective of what little Nana had to share, on every Sunday visit we were treated to the most delicious homemade meals. As we entered the apartment building, our nose would saunter in the direction of her door following the delights of fresh tomato sauce drifting through the cracks— all made for our favorite ravioli and meatballs. Something as simple as an ice cream soda with 7-Up was made extra special when she bought us straws with spoons attached. They were color coded so all six of us would have our own, and don't think she didn't remember each one of our colors. As youngsters, we never understood what "poor" meant, but we certainly knew about love.

My Nana was the quintessential *Positive Manipulator* and made it easy for her kids to still stay loving toward their dad. She never complained, never said a harsh word about him, and never trash-talked him to his relatives. It wasn't until I was almost 40 that I heard stories of abuse in her marriage to him. In fact, I was probably the only person she ever revealed these secrets to. Nana was – and still is at 93 – class all the way. However, my mom and her sister have never forgotten what their dad did to them. Although they forgave much and still care for him and his needs to this day – he's 94 – they live with the scars of their youth and the knowledge that he was not concerned enough about their welfare to support them.

"I have such regret," my mom says of her childhood. "I will never under-stand it. Just because we were from a divorced home, why couldn't he have still acted like a father?" That question lingered throughout my mother's entire life, and the repercussions were felt and are still being passed down to the next two generations of children. In the end, he may believe he got away with not having to give his ex-wife money, but did he really get away with anything? If you consider the *emotional* cost, then not paying didn't pay off.

RELIEVE YOUR CHILD'S GUILT

The judicial system is flawed and run by people who, like any other indus-try, sometimes have their own agenda, flippant moods, ethics and beliefs. We all have seen non-custodial fathers and full-custody mothers who live like paupers because of unfair settlements. It destroys the children to see one parent or another doing poorly. Since divorce is so draining monetarily, it is imperative that each party consistently surveys what is fair to every member of the family, most especially the children. How they perceive each of their parent's lifestyles is of prime importance. If one parent is living high while the other is suffering, the disparity will instigate many negative emotions. Nothing registers more on a child's guilt monitor than seeing one parent having more than the other. Balance is best now for all involved. If you start to lament, "But it's my money!" remember, you don't really own anything in this world. It is all borrowed.

ROD'S STORY

Rod was a tenant of mine and lived in a cute but small one-bedroom apart-ment I had in Oyster Bay, New York. He had a good job and made decent money, but had four children to support, so a small unit was the best he could do. At first I was hesitant to rent to him because his child support was so incredibly high. In fact, it was so extreme and above what the nor-mal rates were, I questioned him on it. It seemed he lost big in a legal bat-tle, and I am not sure how, but he was committed to paying well over his means for the next decade in child support and maintenance. I rented to him anyway, feeling terrible for his plight and, since he had great references who were mutual friends, hoped it would be okay. He managed to pay the rent each month, but each occasion I had to see him, he looked awful, often sick and aging faster than any man I had ever seen. I knew how money created stress in one's life, but this was taking it to the max. He was only 40 years old and looked 60.

One day I asked him how it was going. He told me that his ex-wife was asking for more and more money and he was now working three jobs. With four kids, I am sure she had her woes, but she didn't work and the strain of trying to support two households was deteriorating his health, not to mention his spirit. Occasionally I would see his children when they came to visit him and their faces seemed so dismal and depressed. This family definitely had issues, but little did they know, their lives were about to get even worse. A short time later, Rod secured another place that was even smaller and less expensive. I couldn't imagine how he could manage that with four children visiting on the weekends, but he did. We lost touch, but I couldn't help thinking about him and how the stress must have been taking its toll. A year went by and I ran into a mutual acquaintance of ours. I questioned her about Rod and she looked at me with concern. "You didn't hear?" she asked. "Rod died a few months ago." She must have seen by the look on my ashen face that I was in shock. "It was sudden." She said as she grabbed my arm. "No one really knew he was sick until it was too late."

IS IT WORTH FIGHTING OVER?

Bertrand Russell states, *"If there were in the world today any large number of people who desired their own happiness more than they desired the unhappiness of others, we could have a paradise in a few years."* Oh how true this statement is! Many people would rather take away from their former spouse and concentrate on what they can do to retaliate, rather than concentrating on getting their own life in order. During my interviews with divorcing moms and dads, I have heard it all, from men who give everything, to men who feel justified to give almost nothing. I listened intently to women who felt they deserved more and more, and those who got zero dollars and needed to chase after dead-beat dads. All these stories have one thing in common: There was a fair and equitable way to deal with each situation, but one or both parties – and, possibly, their attorneys – refused to be reasonable. In the end, all suffered, most especially the children.

In my struggle to get support, I felt humiliated and debased. One day I finally gave up, resigning to the fact that I was on my own to deal with my children's financial future. It was a man I was in a relationship with that set me straight after my bemoaning when he bluntly stated, "Dee, get over it! The more you whine about it, the worse it gets! Just deal with it!" He was frustrated for me because he *did* do right by his kids by supporting them properly, and they and his ex wanted for nothing. It was really hard for me to hear those words, but he was so right about all of it, especially my whining. We all get going on the little pity parties we create for ourselves, but eventually; we need to do what we have to do. And the truth is, we didn't want for anything either. Fair or unfair, with their father's help or without it, somehow the kids and I always managed to get what we needed. There may be a point in time, however, when one parent is not living up to the divorce decree and the other parent may have to ask the question; "What should I do about it? Fight? Go to court?"

PEACE AT ANY PRICE

Sometimes the courtroom is our best recourse, but I have found that the more we fight, the less energy we have to find ways to remedy the situation. I decided long ago that I would not legally battle for money because of the repercussions that might ensue. In the early years, I was afraid of how my ex would handle it, and I didn't want the stress related to those fears. More importantly, I didn't want to cause a rift in his relationship with the children or myself. Fighting through the legal system would have made him into an enemy. That was contraindicative to my goal of remaining loving. "Peace at any price" became my mantra although this attitude, to diligent suit filers I have interviewed, is deemed a cop out. In the end, I truly felt more empowered as a woman by not going to court. I took on the role of chief breadwinner and put my energy into being a provider instead of a litigant. I am not against using the legal system, but I am a proponent of self-preservation. Going to court can be harrowing, expensive and doesn't always give you what you want. The system is admittedly overwhelmed and the people in it making the decisions that determine your family's welfare have their own ethics and beliefs and can't possibly know all the nuances of each case they are presented with. With all of this to consider, we have to ask the question, "Is there more to lose emotionally than gain financially?"

Hon. Elaine Jackson Stack, retired Justice of the New York State Supreme Court who handled matrimonial matters for eight years, offers this advice: *"The major issues to be dealt with — money and custody — require the parties to be rational, thoughtful, and civil with each other if they are to decide these issues themselves. If the court becomes involved, the litigants will find that matters of how the family will live post-divorce is placed in the hands of a stranger to their lives. I urge couples to seek mediation or other alternatives to litigation in an effort to find ways to resolve their disputes. The absence of frivolous motions made to the court will also speed their cases to resolution. It may be necessary to turn to the courts, however, if agreements or orders dealing with child support and maintenance are not followed. In tough economic times, modifications of such orders are often sought, and without agreement of both parties, will involve the court's efforts to seek a just outcome."*

When asked what she takes into consideration when "seeking a just outcome," the Judge was unwavering. A "what do you need, not what do you want" approach was always used in her courtroom.

The other scenario for the courtroom warrants even more parental cooperation. Judge Stack continues: *"In the issue of custody, the choices of sole, legal custody (with liberal access by the non-custodial parent), joint custody (with spheres of influence), or joint custody shaped as shared time (50-50 access allocation), are all possibilities for parents. Providing spheres of influence allows the non-custodial parent to continue to be a part of their children's lives even if they live separately. The outcome should be determined by both parties, who have put their egos behind them and sought a resolution best for their children, or it will be by the court, which seldom orders joint or shared custody."*

Judge Stack admits to favoring a 50/50 split of time between parents whenever possible. She also prefers "spheres of decision" that give each parent the ability to decide independently on issues they may have expertise in. "For instance," she explains, "if one parent is a teacher, they should have final say in any disagreement involving education. It shouldn't be up to the court to decide what school a child should attend." Judge Stack cautions that this kind of agreement would require a comprehensive contract to be drawn up initially, but in the long run, she believes it would keep people from continually filing grievances that would further cram the system.

The real truth is, no matter whether you decide to fight legally or not, the kids may still suffer. With the issue of money, if one parent doesn't provide, the kids lose respect for them forever and the kids have to carry around the stigma of not being taken care of for the rest of their lives. If you do fight, you may create a war and that generates a ton of negativity, but it may force the dead-beat parent to do his or her share. In the end, does this help the kids? The answer is sometimes yes, sometimes no, depending on all the circumstances and family dynamics. With custody disputes, Judge Stack tells us the courts generally favor the mother and judgments that go against the norm are usually only impacted by evidence of domestic violence. So without this evidence, does a dad have a chance of being awarded custody? Discussion on whether children should always be raised by the mother could fill up another book, but I will make one comment: The idea that one sex can parent better than another might be proven one day to be as ridiculous a notion as believing the Earth is flat. My belief is that there is never a hard and fast rule so how can there be a hard and fast ruling?

Whatever you decide to do, as a mom or dad, think about and ask yourself this question: "Is it worth it?" If you aren't sure, then ask yourself another question: "Even if it is the right thing to do, is it the *best* thing to do?" Many people feel justified to fight – after all, there are laws, but that doesn't always mean it is the best solution. Today, fortunately, there is the option of mediation that wasn't available to me in the early 90s. A local mediator offers advice to divorcing couples when he explains that law is about winning and losing. His objective is to get every family member to feel as if they have amicably reached an agreement, not that they have lost or won a fight.

This is a wonderful notion, but how do we achieve fairness without the legal system? Again, let's go back to the coffee table scenario and amicably decide who gets what. With a mediator, most couples can come to conclusions without going to court. Judge Stack hopes that all states pass laws that require arbitration by couples before they can enter a courtroom. Although she hopes that the new genre of mediator has a law degree, some believe it is better to have a background in counseling. Since only 20% of divorce cases brought before mediators are uncontested – that is, both sides agree to end the marriage – that leaves 80% of cases in which one partner may not want the divorce.

Someone who does not want to end a relationship will usually drag things out and make it difficult to settle. In these cases, having a background in conflict resolution is important. Being an attorney, however, makes it simpler to explain and handle legal issues during a session. Either way, I am in agreement with Judge Stack: Settling family issues out of the courtroom, peacefully and by family members, not a third party, is the way to go. I am also of the belief that mediators should be attorneys, but am wondering if they shouldn't have a strong background in psychology or social work as well. If the country is moving toward forced mediation, I personally would love to see a new type of accreditation that incorporates conflict resolution as an adjunct to a traditional law degree.

"Why should I settle with that witch!" said the divorcing man to his attorney. The attorney looked straight into the eyes of his stubborn client and said, "Would you rather pay for my son's college education, or yours?"

Many of us know of divorcing couples who fight until the end, literally, expending all of their financial resources to keep each other from getting any assets. This always makes me scratch my head in bewilderment. If you are one of these people, what are you thinking? At one time you took care of your spouse in one way or another. You have children together and you still have responsibility for their welfare. Why would you give away your money to a lawyer or firm you have no stake in?

If you are in the process of divvying up your assets, monetary or otherwise, take a look at what you are really losing. Do the math in your head without any animosity in your heart, then ask yourself, who is making out better – you and your family or your attorney? Although there are many fair and decent attorneys out there, divorces are set up nowadays to be an ongoing process and money-making affair. Do you really want to *buy* into that? According to Judge Stack, counties and municipalities have never been more prepared to help with a do-it-yourself divorce. If you combine this with mediation, do you really need to blow your retirement on your split? Or would you rather give generously and have the money or, at the very least, the energy and time you would have wasted on fighting?

I will tell you with most certainty from my own experience and that of my coaching clients and friends; those of us who gave and walked away, made it back ten-fold and never looked back. My divorce cost me $1,200. I gave all that I could in assets, and we split any money we had in half. I asked for child support, specifically what I knew was the legal percentage for two kids, and I never even fought for what we owed in debts because I knew it was easier to just pay them.

I also knew without a doubt, that if I went the other way and fought for what more I could get, I would be taking away precious energy I didn't want to expend. Instead, I went into what I call "thrival mode" and amped up my efforts in the construction industry. With very little experience and no schooling, I became a successful salesperson and consultant, using whatever skills I had to earn what was needed for the kids. I learned this behavior thankfully from my Nana, but at a young age, a professor at Long Island University enhanced my attitude further when he encouraged me to read "Think and Grow Rich" by Napoleon Hill. That book and its teachings brought me to a whole new level of earning potential.

THE LAWS OF THE UNIVERSE

A life changer, the book details the laws of the universe, most especially the Law of Attraction. You may know of this concept from a book and movie called "The Secret," but may I tell you that Mr. Hill was one of the first to so elaborately explain these laws. I tried to absorb the concepts he wrote about, but in my 20s, I had much less awareness of the world. Suffice it to say, I probably understood less than half of it. I read it through, however, and managed to integrate what I did learn into my everyday life.

Many years later while writing an article for a trade magazine on how to attract money, I went back to his book to find a quote. As I searched through its pages, I re-read many chapters. To my surprise, I understood everything he was saying and had been incorporating all of it for years! It would seem that with the right intention and a little time to help our minds come to conclusions, we have the capacity to absorb, even when we can't fully comprehend. Still, the main message he conveyed was clear, then and now, through hundreds of reprints of his work and over 10 million copies sold: There are laws that lead to fortune. He writes, *The Earth on which you live, you, yourself, and every other material thing are the result of evolutionary change, through which microscopic bits of matter have been organized and arranged in an orderly fashion. Moreover — and this statement is of stupendous importance – this Earth, every one of the billions of individual cells of your body, and every atom of matter, began as an intangible form of energy."*

What he is saying is that money is intangible, like an idea or invention, until you give it physical life, or in other words, manifest it. He continues by saying, *"Desire is thought impulse! Thought impulses are forms of energy. When you begin with the thought impulse to desire to accumulate money, you are drafting into your service the same "stuff" that nature used in creating this Earth, and every material form in the universe, including the body and brain in which the thought impulses function."*

If you have issues with money, and you doubt your innate ability to bring it in, read the book, and then if you want to take it a little further, familiarize yourself with Jerry and Ester Hicks and their CDs, books and DVDs about Abraham and the universal laws of attraction. All are lessons you can use to attract what you need and want to make a new life for yourself and your children. I utilized these teachings and was able to retire from my sales career to pursue my dream of being a pro-bono wellness advocate. Although we never lived extravagantly, using these laws and believing in my ability to bring in what I needed, kept us afloat financially and then some. My kids and I always paid our bills and had what we needed to live comfortably and securely.

RE-DIRECT YOUR PRECIOUS ENERGY

Instead of fighting tooth and nail to get every tooth and nail from him, I put the energy I would have used in court into my business. I *Positively Manipulated* any remnants of resentment and any feelings of entitlement into determination to succeed. It wasn't an "I will show him" attitude either. It was more like, "It's gotta get done, so put the nose to the grindstone and get going." This attitude was validated for me when I read Mr. Hill's words on Page 154: *"Some men who have accumulated great fortunes did so because of necessity. They developed the habit of persistence, because they were so closely driven by circumstances that they had to become persistent."*

Again, I am not a saint, but I am realistic, and I understand that holding onto negative energy about money, like wishing I had more, or being angry at him for paying less, precluded me from bringing it in, and I wasn't about to let that happen. People who understand this concept live happier, healthier – and wealthier!—lives. But don't take my word for it. Here is a passage from Phylameana lila Desy: "*When we focus on having less, then we create that experience for ourselves. When we focus on "I hate my job" (for instance) then we will never notice the aspects of our employment that might be satisfying. Basically, just wanting something isn't going to bring that to us when we continue to obsess on the not having of that something. All we will experience is "not having" and will be ultimately blocking our true desires.*"

Understanding this and using the Law of Attraction can free you of dependency! Imagine what life would be like not having to rely on anyone for anything. Some women make me chuckle when I hear them say their life would be so much better with more money, exclaiming, "I'm going to make sure my next marriage will be to a multi-millionaire." My remark to them is, "By the time you find one and figure out how to land him, you could make a million on your own!" Start now to stop worrying about what you may be doing without and instead desire what you want. Then watch as the money comes right in!

BOOMERANG!

On the contrary, the Law of Return also applies. If we deny our former spouse and family of what they need, we can't expect goodness to come back to us. Taking or withholding from our kids is a sin against our own souls and a crime against them and society. We will never come out ahead if we don't heed this message.

Loose tongues are worse than wicked hands.

Jewish Proverb

COMMANDMENT VI
THOU SHALT KEEP THY OPINIONS TO THYSELF!

Don't pit family, friends, and especially the children against your future ex. Remember what goes around, comes around. No matter what one spouse is saying, two wrongs will never make the situation better. Keep your nose clean at all times and eventually the truth will come out. It always does.

If you are a grandparent or relative of a divorcing family, you may be at your wits end witnessing what is transpiring. Please know you have some power to steer your grandchildren (nieces/nephews/siblings) in the right direction. You have unconditional love on your side and those kids need you more than ever. Offer them a safe haven and some semblance of normalcy. In the dedication of this book, I give credit to my mom for being such a positive influence on my life and an instrument of peace through my divorce. She generated happy memories and constant and consistent love to my children, bringing them carefully through all their tough times. By always remaining neutral and nonjudgmental toward my ex, irrespective of what was going on, she created a safe haven that they feel comforted by to this day.

HOLDING YOUR TONGUE

How often do we hear someone trash their former spouse so vehemently you wonder how love could ever have existed between them? Some people can't even say their ex's name without slanting their brows in anger or snarling in disgust. When you are a parent though, you need to remember something of primary importance; the person you may have such disdain for is the father or mother of your child. You may also want to remember that you chose this person, you married him/her, and you vowed to spend the rest of your life with them. To trash them now in front of the very people who watched you take those vows would say more about your lack of discernment than it would about their faults.

Many divorcees have come to me, revealing horror stories of what their ex is spewing to extended family members and the children. I have also witnessed it during coaching sessions, and I have to say, the hair goes up on the back of my neck. It is so vile to hurt children in this way! I am happy to say that my children were not tainted by negative stories about either of us during their young lives. To my husband's credit, he did not tell tall tales or speak ill of me to the kids, nor did I report my account of my life with him. Although I admit to both of us not being able to control every word out of our mouths, in the long run, keeping our opinions about each other and the downfall of the marriage to ourselves helped our kids see truth, not slanted versions of our own realities.

But, let's for a minute put ourselves in the shoes of the children who are not so blessed and try to empathize with their plight. At any age under 18, 19 or even 21, they are impressionable. They are trying to understand the how and why of what led to the divorce. Depending on the child, they are taking on some of the blame. They are picturing their future and the battles that will ensue at every holiday, birthday, religious ceremony and graduation. It creates a lifelong sense of instability for a child to hear terrible things about their mom and dad.

Slander slays three persons: the speaker, the spoken to, and the spoken of.— Hebrew Proverb

In one of the first chapters of this book I wrote about how people would do almost anything for their child if they were sick, or lost, or trapped somewhere, but sometimes, something as simple as keeping one's mouth shut is too big a task. Telling your children awful things about their parent is called parental alienation, and is considered emotional abuse. It isn't necessary and is definitely harmful. It should be a priority to make your children see the goodness in everyone, most especially their parents. This is when *Positive Manipulation* becomes crucial!

UNDERSTANDING THE IMPACT OF OUR WORDS AND ACTIONS

We all know the results of stress, fighting, and negative behavior and how it plays a critical role in our ability to stay healthy and prosper emotionally. To believe that parent alienation, monetary worries, name calling and constant fighting has no detrimental effect on the future welfare of our children should render us blind and inane. EVERYTHING, good or bad, affects a child!

Recently I heard Archbishop Timothy M. Dolan of New York express the joy of his childhood and how he was cherished and adored by both his parents. He said, "The greatest blessing one could have is to be brought up in a loving family." Who doesn't agree with this? Yet many will admonish altruistic parental policies when painful emotion is involved. Although I tried to manipulate myself through many a fight, I spewed a few in my time. When this occurred, anger, hurt, frustration and fear played the lead in the formation of negative words I used to address the father of my children.

No matter in what environment a child is raised, I don't believe anything can have more of a profound effect on their self-esteem than words. It is not just the words we use to address them that has the most impact; what we say and do to their other parent leaves just as deep an impression. It is so important to understand that how we handle ourselves and interact with our former spouse during the years of our divorce will influence our children for a lifetime. Realize that their little bodies contain DNA from both of you, which means when you put down or undermine a child's mommy or daddy with insults or harmful adjectives, you alienate a part of them as well.

What example am I setting? This is the question I asked myself after scolding Matthew for grabbing and twisting his little sister's arm and calling her a horribly nasty word. All this because she broke the lock on his door and "rearranged" his room. After yelling, I ended the tirade with, "You are just as mean as your father!" How often do we tell our children not to speak badly of others and then turn around and do the same? It wasn't until I experienced a few "epiphanies" that I truly came to appreciate the negative aftermath that spewing hateful remarks created for my kids. In time, manipulating my words and holding my tongue was not a struggle; it became easier and easier – even rewarding – as I felt the positive energy enlivening me and the children.

In a recent televised sermon about raising our young ones, Pastor Joel Osteen stated, *"There are incredible powers in our words."* If this is true, then when we speak against our former spouse, who are we hurting? When we name call or use negative words to describe a child's parent, are we defining them (our ex) or ourselves? In order to counteract the negativity of divorce, we need to, (and I will borrow this from Joel Osteen), *"speak blessings and release favor into their future."* We all have to agree: It is the only way we can raise them successfully.

MONKEY SEE, MONKEY DO

And there is this other aspect we must constantly remind ourselves of: forgiveness. How can we teach our children about this incredible virtue if we do not exhibit it in our own lives? To taint the character of another person because of what we perceive they have done to us is not going to help anyone, most especially the children. Instead, we must continually try to **Positively Manipulate** those negative thoughts by finding some quality we can hang onto in order to help our children accept each parent and their gifts. After all, if children believe they come from garbage they will feel like they are made of the same.

Sri Chinmoy says, *"Unconditional love is the connecting link between Earth's ascending face and heaven's descending grace."* When there is abuse, adultery, thievery, or any other incredibly negative behavior that caused the divorce, it is particularly difficult to find the grace to forgive. There may not be one single cell in your brain that you can convince to change. Let me give you some food for thought: The more negativity you carry around, the more unhappiness *you* feel. It helps no one, least of all the person you are angry with, to stay rigid about this aspect of healing.

Forgiveness allows for inner peace. It promotes and even instigates love within your heart and no matter what you believe now, if you try it once, you will never go back to harboring emotions like anger and resentment again. And something more to consider; you may not be married anymore and that is cause for sorrow, but you can turn it around and believe that you are now free of someone who in the past had the ability to hurt you so badly. Can you find happiness in that?

UNDERSTANDING WHAT FEMININE AND MASCULINE QUALITIES TEACH US

I can't speak for every young girl, but I remember as a child fighting with my sisters about who was going to marry Daddy. We would play-argue over who would make a better "wife" for him. Was it me because I could cook hamburgers and loved to fish, or was it Dawn because she enjoyed Carvel as much as he did? I can't imagine what it would have been like to hear terrible stories of the man I admired. Of course, we grew out of this phase, but the memory remains with me, because it expresses just how profoundly we adore our parents.

If you are a woman reading this book and had a father growing up, did you know that you developed your femininity through watching his behavior toward you? If you are a man who was raised by your mother, did you know you learned how to respond to women through the way she treated you as a boy? Most of us don't realize or want to admit how much of our personality was gleaned from our parents.

When you were young, did you ever hear yourself say, "When I have kids, things will be different!" Ideals, traits, morals, habits and little idiosyncrasies are either adopted by us or deleted from our persona and lifestyle depending on what we liked and didn't like about our parents. But how we feel about ourselves and interact with the opposite sex is directly related to how we were treated and loved by our parent of the opposite sex. In other words, I learned how to *act* as a mother and woman by watching my mom, but how I felt about *being* a woman was directly related to how my dad treated me and how he showed and didn't show love. His influence and opinion of me had a direct effect on my relationship choices and most especially, how I allowed men to treat me.

When we disenchant our children towards one parent or another, we deprive them of learning, growing, and sharing in their unique childhood experience. Even though we may believe our former spouse is wrong for us, how many of us really believe they are wrong for our children as well? It is my opinion, gained from life experience and practical knowledge, that very few parents are so awful they should be denied a prominent place in their children's lives, free of malice and alienation. Yes, there are cases when visitation and contact is limited for good reason, but even when a parent is mentally ill, alcoholic, drug addicted or abusive, there is usually some part, albeit small, the ill parent can play. In fact, sometimes they exhibit for our kids *what not to do* better than any life lesson we could teach!

In any case, the healthier parent does not have the right to slander their ex with more terrible stories and name-calling. When one parent is in bad shape, think about how the child feels. Shouldn't the healthy parent help the child find something positive to hang onto? Living with the stigma attached to having a parent that does really bad things will surely become a lifelong issue. When it comes time to deal with those issues and tell the children the truth about their parent, does it have to come with horrible adjectives attached? This is a crucial step in the *Positive Manipulation* process. We need to be able to find good things to say about our former spouse, even if they are *not so good* so we can build our kids up, not knock them down.

JOE AND JUDY

Judy has Borderline Personality Disorder (BPD) and she and her husband cannot be in the same room together, or even on the phone for that matter, without name calling and exhibiting completely horrendous behavior. Their children are present for most fights and neither parent can stop themselves, constantly blaming the other for starting it or fueling it.

When the dueling starts, their three children run and hide, burying their little heads under pillows or a nearby security blanket, huddling as if they were in a bomb shelter. Unfortunately, nothing helps to drown out the hateful words their parents are spewing at one another. Strangely, the husband blames his future ex-wife's behavior on her disorder, but then what is his excuse? I wonder how he can recall her tirades and incredibly bad decisions and fault her for them, but not take responsibility for what he is doing to the children as well. What messages are these parents sending out by calling each other whore, bastard, prick, and the like? How is this helping their situation or healing their own pain? How do they expect their children to not continue on the tradition in their own lives? What kind of behavior is it teaching them?

Most people would not train their kids to go into the world with bad attitudes and hatred, but parents who spew are doing just that. In fact, a volatile household is the perfect campground for raising an emotionally disturbed child. Would that ever be someone's goal? Instead, I teach clients to counteract negative behavior and help kids to find excuses for what an ill parent has said and done. Acknowledging mental illness can be a God-send for an ailing child. After all, what is the alternative?

It's Never Too Late

Joe and Judy's extended family cannot stop them. The police cannot stop them. Even their children's crying and begging can't stop them. Their family is doomed emotionally if these parents cannot get it together. The good news is, if they finally choose to, they could reverse the damage by stopping the insanity and *Positively Manipulating* their hatred for one another into a mutual love for their children. Forgiveness is always an option and it is never too late to turn the damage around, no matter what was said in the past!

Irrespective of what someone has done to you, whether it is cheating, stealing, beating, or any other form of abuse, there is never a reason to drag your children into your emotional warfare. Remember, TRASHING HIM OR HER CANNOT TAKE AWAY YOUR ANGER OR PAIN! It can only produce more of the same horrible throbbing and negativity for you and your kids. And trust me, later on you will deal with even more woe as your child grows into a young adult with an inability to handle their emotions (like anger, anxiety, or fear) towards you and the world. Along with the animosity will come depression, low self esteem, and self worth as well. All this negativity generated by a parent's inability to *Positively Manipulate* their own mouth. How very tragic. How avoidable!

"Bite your tongue!" must have come from a grandparent witnessing the demise of a family. I am convinced of it. If there was ever an instance that made this statement viable, it is this one. Hold onto those hateful remarks or they will come back to you. And if you are already doing your best and the other party won't stop, don't worry. The dichotomy of positive and negative you are creating won't go unnoticed, and the children will benefit from your behavior. Lead by example and know you are doing the right thing, no matter how hard it seems to maintain your positive performance right now. One day, they will thank you for it.

MATTHEW'S WEDDING

When it comes to divorce, opinions fly from all sources, most especially acquaintances who think they know a couple's entire story simply by observing. In trying to decide which side to be on, most people form their own opinions about why a loved one, family member, or friend ended up divorced. This is tragic; because most often, no one, not even the participants themselves, are aware of all the factors that instigated their break-up. This reality hit home for me when an unfortunate incident occurred at my son's wedding. A few weeks before the big day, it came time for the mother/son dance number to be selected, and it was important to me to put some thought into what message the song should convey. I was excited to be honored, but while basking in the glow of being mother of the groom, sadness also came over me. I recognized that I could never take all the credit for mothering him and it weighed heavy on my heart.

Flitting through my mind were memories of all the times my mother came to my son's aid time and again. She was the nurse who held his head when he threw up. She was the cook who made him chicken broth after he was done. She was the chauffeur who ran out at the spur of the moment to pick him up at day care when I was stuck in traffic, or make it to his school recital when I had to work. The thought of not acknowledging her love as a grandmother was actually painful to me. I didn't feel I could take the honor without also paying homage to her participation. After thinking about it, I went to my son (and his future bride Jessica) and asked for advice. "How would you feel, Matt, if I dedicated part of my dance with you to Nana?"

Both responded well, so I had to assume they knew exactly what energy and spirit of goodness was behind my request.

On the day of the wedding, when it came time for us to enter the dance floor, the DJ announced that the mother of the groom had a favor to ask. After retrieving the microphone, I began to tell the story of being a young mother and needing to work many crazy hours to run the family store. "It takes a village to raise a child," I reminded everyone, "and in Matt's case, there were many people who loved and cared for him, but there was one special person I would like to tell you about."

I went on to recant a story that to this day can still make me teary. "I remember distinctly, arriving at Mom's house one day after work to pick up little Matthew. After announcing that I was 'home,' I didn't hear a response, so I followed the TV sounds coming from the basement. I wanted to surprise them, so I peeked around the corner of the stairwell and saw a sight that would change my life forever. There was my mom, standing over her ironing board, pressing one of my dad's shirts."

I paused for a second to compose myself and stooped a bit so I could gesture with my hand, about 24 inches from the ground. "Matthew was only this big, but there he was, standing by her side at three years old, with his miniature ironing board and plugged in toy iron, trying so hard to take the creases out of a pillow case. My heart sank as I looked at them. It was at that moment, even at the age of 25, that I realized what a profound event was taking place. My child was being taken care of in a way I could never realize. Because of his Nana, he would get a special kind of motherly love I had no time or energy to give."

The audience was hushed as I continued my speech and I finally ended by asking for their help in getting my mom to join Matthew on the dance floor while we honored her participation in his rearing. Everyone applauded and she and my son swayed arm in arm to "You Raise Me Up" by Josh Groban. Halfway through the song, I grabbed my stepfather and handed him over to my mom while I joined Matthew and we all finished the dance together. It was a cherished moment for her and me, and one my mother says she will never forget.

As I left the dance floor to find my way back to the table, my friend Rudy came to escort me, and as we were talking, I was approached by one of my ex-husband's guests. Barefoot and stern-faced, she interrupted our conversation by asking if we could talk. Rudy excused himself and the second he turned away, she blurted, "Do you think that is fair what you just did?" "I'm sorry?" I questioned, with what must have been an incredulous look on my face. "What are you talking about?" "That speech you gave," she continued, "do you know what you did? Your husband is over at his family table inconsolable because of what you said!"

Part of me did not comprehend what she was saying. Apparently, the accolades I gave my mother were taken as an affront by my ex. I was floored by this! Truthfully, this person was never tactful in the past, so I wasn't surprised that she had the nerve, but what I didn't understand was how honoring my mother during a mother/son dance could have any ill effect on him. What does the father of the groom have to do with a mother-of-the-groom dance? Was his family that *in the dark* about how I had to raise my children? Didn't anyone understand how much I owed my mother? I wasn't laying blame on anyone by giving her credit. I was acknowledging what an incredible woman she was and how wonderfully my son was reared because of all the love she gave. If anything, I was undermining my own ability to mother, fully admitting to not being there for him when he needed me!

I was shocked, hurt, and angry at the audacity of this woman to interfere, but mostly I wanted to shout to the entire room what I really went through all those years. Anger mixed with pain welled up in me and was almost unbearable. I gestured with my hand as if to dismiss her and then turned away saying, "Please, you don't have any idea what you are talking about!" She physically grabbed my arm, trying to hold me back. At that moment, I looked at her sternly, pulled my arm away, and trying not to lose it completely, walked away while forcing back a rush of tears.

When I coach clients through incidents in their lives, I usually provoke a healing by asking them to ask themselves, "What is the lesson here?" It didn't take me long to realize how paying tribute to my mother was necessary for me because I needed to acknowledge what I wasn't able to give Matthew while he was growing up. And yes, that was an affront to his father. We didn't have a stellar family life. Although I kept an immaculate house, tried to keep nourishing food in the fridge and managed to be a den mother when he was in Cub Scouts, for the most part, he was a latch-key kid with lots of drama to deal with on a daily basis. I can't imagine that my ex was angry or hurt about what I did for my mom that day. Given the opportunity, I believe he would have done the same. Instead, I think the reality of the previous 27 years hit him. We didn't give our kids a cookies-and- milk upbringing. We didn't provide them with a peaceful home with lots of weekend family outings. They had tough issues to deal with and lots of uncomfortable situations to get through. No, it wasn't the mother-son tribute that was causing emotions to run high. I can imagine he was feeling as guilty as I was for the lack of normalcy our children endured.

Still, family and friends formed opinions that day and the negative energy endured for some time after. When my daughter graduated from high school, I was scorned by his family members during the ceremony. The most unfortunate aspect of judgment, however, is something no one thinks about, and that is how the children will react. When someone judges or ridicules a child's parent, they may alienate themselves right out of the child's life. Unless we absolutely know the whole story, (which is impossible unless we were there for every incident) do we deserve to judge? And even then, *who are we* to judge?

EENIE, MEANY, MINEY, MOE

When family and friends take sides during the divorce process it is usually so they can choose one to remain friendly with. Most people find it difficult to juggle. When I left my husband, I decided not to expose the specifics of our marital woes to anyone. Instead of trying to divvy up the friendships, I walked away from everyone. Looking back, I am not sure it was right or wrong to leave myself totally alone to start over, but I couldn't stand the thought of being judged and, believe it or not, I didn't want him to be judged either. Perhaps I left myself more prone to ridicule by not talking, but I was ashamed, embarrassed and most of all, exhausted.

People formed their opinions early on though, and I never tried to change anyone's mind thinking it was futile and unfair. To this day many of those mutual friends have no idea why I divorced him or what I endured. My hope in staying silent was that they would try to stay nonaligned, but that theory back-fired as some sided with him and actually became hostile toward me. Because of this, my children became uncomfortable with certain people, making life just that much tougher for them. Children who are going through a divorce deserve peace in their lives. Taking sides and judging either one of their parents just isn't fair and it is definitely unnecessary. We all need to remember this great adage from Wayne Dyer, *"When you judge others, it doesn't define who they are, it defines who you are."*

"Keeping score of old scores and scars, getting even and one-upping, always makes you less than you are."

Malcolm Forbes

COMMANDMENT VII
THOU SHALT KEEP THE PAST IN THE PAST

While going forward, there is no reason to go back. When things get really heated, **don't rehash old stuff**. Keep to the subject at hand. Constantly reiterate to yourself and the other person that you want to solve the problem you are having. The old fights never get resolved and that is probably why you are getting the divorce in the first place. Use your new *Positive Manipulation* tools; validate your ex with the "I understand what you are saying" statement and go on to the present.

CONFESSIONS OF A RECALL-A-HOLIC

I have to admit, I am famous for this one as any man in my former life would attest to. During my marriage and in other relationships, I would continuously recount every episode until I was red with rage. Of course, this got me nowhere and it was usually at some point during my "how can I ever forget when you...!" diatribe that my partner's ears would flop over. Truthfully, I have a notion that women do this more than men do. It is as if we rehash our pain through every episode we encounter and they all seem to trigger the same emotion. So when a current episode feels just like a past one, we tend to think it is necessary to recall them all! Not helpful, but we do it anyway. Here's the thing though; you are not married anymore, so there is nothing to be gained by bringing up old hurts and pains. Instead, save it for your therapist and if you want to take it a step further, use the negative episodes to figure out what common denominator they all carry, namely you!

LEARNING FROM *THEIR* MISTAKES

On my life journey, I realized I was attracting the same hurt and pain from every man I was in a relationship with. And that notion was confirmed some years ago after spending time researching American Indian Medicine. In the book, "Medicine Cards" by Jamie Sams and David Carson, the authors describe how Native Americans use animals to recognize their strengths and frailties, and they turn to "animal medicine" to heal. There is a delightful story about a rabbit that brought so much clarity to me, I have to share it.

At one time, the rabbit was considered courageous and bold, but after encountering a witch, he was cursed with attracting fear into his realm. Since then, the rabbit has been referred to as the "Fear Caller." While peacefully grazing in a field, the rabbit will look up and see an eagle. Sams and Carson write, *"He goes out and shouts, 'Eagle, I am afraid of you!' If Eagle does not hear him, Rabbit calls louder, 'Eagle, stay away from me!' Eagle, now hearing Rabbit, comes and eats him."* This story sounded crazy to me until the authors revealed the ancient wisdom behind the tale. *"As the story shows, Rabbit medicine people are so afraid of tragedy, illness, disaster and of 'being taken,' that they call those very fears to them to teach them lessons. The key note here is: what you resist will persist! What you fear most is what you will become."* Being a student of energy, I recognized the law of attraction right away, and then it was seconds later when I realized my long-time fear of emotional abandonment was almost luring in, energetically and unwittingly, men who were masters at emotional escape.

The picture was becoming crystal clear: Since every fight I had was over the same issues with each man, it would trigger the pain from all past issues that were never resolved. When I found my own weakness and realized I was the common denominator in each of these relationships, I decided I needed to change myself and work on those very issues that were keeping me from staying in the present. My thought was, "If I want a great guy, I have to be a great woman!" I understand now that if I didn't take responsibility for the annoying habit of rehashing, it would have never changed no matter what man I was with. It became obvious that the *mistakes* they made with me became my lessons to learn from.

EMDR, EFT AND NET

Candace Pert writes in "Molecules of Emotion," *"It's true, we do store some memory in the brain, but by far, the deeper, older messages are stored in the body and must be accessed through the body. Your body is your subconscious mind and you can't heal it by talk alone."*

Many people aren't aware that trauma, even seemingly small issues, felt and dealt with through your life can build up in your body, finding refuge in organs, joints, muscle tissue and most especially cells. No matter how much mental or emotional therapy one undergoes, the physical body will still retain the negative unless a special process of elimination is undertaken.

Over the decades, I had been acutely aware that my own memories of the past were holding me back from being all I could be. After researching for some time, I came up with amazing therapies, such as EMDR, hypnosis, Trauma Release Acupuncture, and of course, Yoga and guided meditation.

EMDR was the first form of therapy I used, which stands for "Eye Movement Desensitization and Reprocessing." It is quite a title for a simple procedure that uses eye movement and/or ear tones to eradicate Post Traumatic Stress Disorder, or PTSD. It affects over 5 million adults nationwide each year and is seen not only in war veterans, but also in disaster victims, police officers, abused women and children – anyone who has suffered a traumatic experience. In my case, it was abuse by men.

In order to break the destructive pattern of PTSD, Dr. Francine Shapiro at the Mental Research Institute in Palo Alto, California, developed this unusual form of therapy. If I remember the story correctly, she discovered the technique while walking one day and recalling a disturbing event. As she strolled, her eyes began to dart back and forth and as they did, she noticed a remarkable decrease in her uneasiness and anxiety. The treatment she ultimately created is done in a therapist's office and is completely benign as you watch a pendulum swing back and forth or listen with a headset to a tape that sends tones to each ear, left then right, repeatedly. As you do this, memories play back as if they were on a video player. They may cause an immediate response from your body, possibly traumatic, but within seconds, the feeling is released as you realize the trauma is no longer taking place because you are in the present, safe and sound.

I remember one visit in particular at which the doctor and I were trying to figure out why I was so terrified of driving up to toll booths. Being in outside sales and having two states as my territory, the need to go over bridges and toll roads was unavoidable, so we made it a point to investigate thoroughly. While comfortably seated in his office and wearing my ear phones, I tried to envision myself going over the Verrazano Bridge in New York and approaching the booth. Immediately, I started to panic and break out in a sweat at the mere thought of pulling up to it. While physically reliving this, my mind recalled a day when my EZ-Pass did not work and I was stuck in the booth for what felt like an eternity while people, including a police officer, honked and yelled at me. The feeling of being trapped and held there was almost too much to bear and my body started to contort, seemingly trying to squeeze its way out of the tight spot. Seeing this, the doctor asked me to describe what was happening and all of a sudden, another scene and feelings of entrapment emerged. It was of me, being held flat against a white wall, huge hands gripping my throat in a chokehold and my feet dangling in the air. Then another picture and sensation came and I was reliving being held down on the ground, arms pinned to my sides, feet and legs unable to move. This flashback should have induced sheer terror, but instead, I saw, I felt, I released. As each memory rolled back, the feeling of dread, claustrophobia, and most especially, terror left my body.

It didn't take long before we realized the connection between my fears of being trapped in a toll booth with incidents of abuse from my past. In fact, it became so obvious to both of us as if it were a completely logical connection. It wasn't *going through* the toll booth that was my problem. It was the potential of getting stuck there and not being able to pass through the gate that was causing me to have severe fright. The mere suggestion of not being capable of escaping, stuck in my car in a tiny confined space with a gate blocking my exit, was my issue. Within seconds of making the connection, my angst magically disappeared and thereafter I had no concern with passing through the tolls. It was a miracle and a newfound freedom from feelings of entrapment! Of course, this makes sense now, but at the time, it seemed totally illogical that a grown woman would have such distress over something as innocuous as a toll lane. This is the way post-traumatic stress works, and fortunately it can be eradicated with minor discomfort through EMDR. Although I found this treatment to be very helpful, after a while, it became so expensive I deemed the anxiety associated with paying the weekly bill to be more painful than the actual traumas! The therapy had its place in my life, though, and I would recommend it to anyone who has been through life-threatening events.

The next forms of therapy came about much later and had more to do with my desire to help others. During my coaching practice, frustration grew over my inability to help certain people get to their next level in healing. Because of negative patterns repeated over and over, no amount of talking or goal orientation I came up with could help them. I used my frustration, however, to ask for help from the Universe. When I did, a specialized practitioner came marching into my life with the answers I had been looking for. This man was a chiropractor who had taken healing to the next level. Combining his knowledge of physiology with a passionate desire to heal, Dr. Fred began his training in three different practices; NET (Neuro Emotional Technique, NEAT (Neuro Emotional Anti-Sabotage Technique) and EFT (Emotional Freedom Technique). Many letters here, but don't be alarmed. The methods are easy to understand and simple to administer by a trained professional, making the job of releasing your past a straightforward task.

YOU CAN RUN, BUT YOU CAN'T HIDE!

When it comes to releasing past pain and redirecting energy – *Positive Manipulation* – the most difficult aspect is acknowledgement. Hiding from our pain is a safety mechanism that makes it easier to deal with. When we have no idea as humans how to handle an event or experience, we go into survival mode. So it makes sense that our bodies would tuck trauma away so we can continue to survive. On a mental and emotional level, we are still triggered by these past events, so trying to become healthy and just live an ordinary life turns into a monumental challenge, instigating the need to Positively Manipulate ourselves back from the negative over and over again.

The techniques this practitioner uses enable him to speak directly to your body without your mental or emotional state interfering with the process. When you can't hide from your traumas any longer, your body will just admit to them and then the real process of healing can occur. By simply asking your body questions and using a technique called applied kinesiology to obtain the answers, he asks you to pinpoint an emotion or current event that is causing reoccurring stress in your life. He then tries to locate the part of the body that emotion is being stored. When he locates it, he identifies what that feeling is (i.e. anger, resentment, fear, abandonment, etc), and then goes on to determine the exact age at which the original emotion may have started.

Once you have full acknowledgement of a trauma spot, he can help release it through body tapping and affirmations. Sounds too simple to be true, but the process works, and I have been undergoing treatments for years now. In addition, I have sent dozens of my clients to Dr. Fred, and they have experienced great success with everything from alleviating a fear of elevators to emotionally healing from sexual abuse. Most recently, I have been experimenting with a new version of these therapies from a book called "The Emotion Code," which is a must-read if you want to facilitate your own healing.

There is no doubt that many marriages and breakups are traumatic enough to cause PTSD-like symptoms, and what I like to call "tiny Ts" or tiny traumas. And even if you are not diagnosed with a specific condition, you undoubtedly harbor all sorts of negative emotions towards your ex, such as resentment, abandonment and possibly guilt that you need to dislodge from your system.

These energy healing therapies have moved me into a new dimension of hope and tranquility. I have released all kinds of emotions that were stuck, some since childhood, and I now see a remarkable difference in how I handle all aspects of my life, most importantly, how I feel about the past. When the painful memories were gone from my body, my mind didn't have the need to talk about them anymore. What a gift, to myself and those around me!

A BROKEN RECORD

If you are on the opposite end of this argument, meaning your ex or other people in your life tend to remind you of the same things you do over and over, you may want to finally sit up and listen. Perhaps you need to dig in and discover if there is something within yourself that may need to change? Listen to their words and use them to discover a facet about yourself that will help get you through the next phase of your life.

WALTER'S STORY

In one of my coaching sessions with Walter, a divorced man in his late 40s, he confessed to constantly being told by every woman he has been with that he was emotionally unavailable. To him, every woman's voice was whining the same old thing: "You never spend enough time with me!" His thoughts were, "I just want to be selfish right now. I want someone who knows I am still there for them, even when I am not there." My advice to him was to examine why he couldn't bring himself to be with the women he supposedly loved, and why he would find any reason to run away. The question posed was, "Where does the need to spend so much time working or having fun with 'the boys' come from?"

I went on to remind him that he would keep attracting more of the same into his life until he changed what is inside of himself. He needed to find out why he was attracted to doting women who wanted more, instead of very independent women who wouldn't care what he was up to. Even better, he needed to figure out why he cannot enjoy being with the women he chooses. In doing this, he can stop blaming these women for being so emotional and needy. The fights he endured during his marriage and subsequent relationships could have been resolved if he decided they had some merit and then took steps to do something about it. Instead, he chooses to believe he will someday find someone who will put up with his lifestyle. Only then will he have found his "perfect woman."

Unfortunately – and fortunately, depending on how you look at it! – we attract exactly what we need to heal. (Again, we need to refer to the nut and bolt theory.) His desire to run is unhealthy and he will keep living the same life, attracting the same kind of women, if he doesn't decide to change and heal what is not working within himself. In fact, this is why the divorce rate for second marriages is higher than the first; we choose to believe the other person is crazy for what they believe instead of giving them the credit for feeling and sensing deficits in us. If we never change ourselves, how can we hope to attract better relationships into our lives in the future?

ENOUGH SAID

No matter what the scenario, rehashing without resolving is not going to work out any issues in your relationship, both past and future. It is about the NOW and if you can finally bring yourself to hear what your ex is saying, maybe you can learn something about him/her and yourself. This in and of itself can release a ton of past pain! Imagine if you can finally see through your own animosity long enough to empathize or better yet, validate him or her? Eckhart Tolle in his book, "The Power of Now," beckons us to *"break the old pattern of present-moment denial and present-moment resistance. Make it your practice to withdraw attention from past and future whenever they are not needed. Step out of the time dimension as much as possible in everyday life."*

Guaranteed, if you can do it, your divorce process will be extraordinary. And after all, you have nothing to lose at this point and everything to gain. Find out what past events are triggering the present pain in yourself and your ex and you release lots of negativity once and for all. There is nothing like cleaning up karmic debt to clear the negative energy you both may have generated, making the next stages of your life what you want, instead of a repeat of the past.

*"It may take a village to raise a child,
but it only takes one child to raise a parent."* **DM**

COMMANDMENT VIII
THOU SHALT NOT USE THY CHILDREN FOR THINE OWN GAIN

No matter how much pain we are in, there is never an excuse for using our children in any way to get what we want from our former spouse. **NEVER, EVER USE THE KIDS!** Don't fight in front of them. Never solicit them to ask their other parent for anything, including information, money or sympathy. Of course, this is a very difficult request, but it is so worth it in the end. Any discussions about important matters should be between the co-parents and the kids should be left out. Even older kids have it rough when one parent continually suggests, "Go ask your father!"

ANOTHER LESSON LEARNED THE HARD WAY

By the 15th year of my divorce, my son was in his late-20s and my daughter was 18. Tired of being the "Bank of Martini," I started to ask my daughter to go to her father for money when she needed it. I couldn't take saying no to her requests and kept thinking to myself, "If we were still together as husband and wife, I would be telling her to ask him. Don't most married couples do this?" Unfortunately, I wasn't thinking about the repercussions.

She was terrified to ask him and I couldn't understand why. During the 27 years we were parents, he never once laid a hand on either child, so what was the big deal? Then one day the realization came to me. She was afraid that he might say no. At her current age, I felt justified to tell her to go to him. He never responded to any requests I had for help, so I had given up long before, but I didn't want Heather to be caught in the middle of that argument. Instead, I asked her as a young woman to talk to her dad about helping with college. Was that so bad? Apparently yes, because it caused her much distress. Looking back, I wasn't taking everything into account. If he gave her money, it could present a healing. But if he refused, it could devastate her self-esteem. My point is, even though she was an adult, children at almost any age do not have the wherewithal to deal with the negativity generated by dueling parents. This isn't the worst aspect of using our kids though. Some of us can't stop our need to know what is going on in our ex-spouses life.

HE COULDN'T HELP HIMSELF

My client Ted confided to me that he couldn't stop himself from prying into his ex's life and using his kids to do it. Every time he had them for the weekend, he would grill each child for info about his former spouse's dating habits, names of friends who came to visit, what she bought for herself, even how she dressed when she went out. He even got his daughter's Facebook password so he could spy. It became evident that he was using his kids to stalk her every move.

The children were pre-teen but sophisticated enough to understand what they were being asked to do. Torn between honoring their dad's request and being loyal to their mom, they became uncomfortable seeing their dad and requested being able to stay home more and more rather than spend time with him. After realizing this, he stopped the inquiries and sought me out for help with his obsession.

Divorce is hard enough for children without having to deal with the negative behaviors of their parents. Confusion is part of their everyday scenario now that we as adults have altered their lives forever. How do we recognize and resolve our own frailties and tendencies in order to keep ourselves from inflicting even more pain on them?

Using *Positive Manipulation* Gets Results

I remember specifically the day I confronted my ex-husband about visitation. It was one year after we had separated and I was rattled by his inability to keep to a routine with the kids. Our agreement specifically stated that he picked them up every Tuesday and Thursday night and every other weekend from Friday after work to Sunday evening after supper. Instead, he skipped most weekday visits and would take them every other Saturday afternoon and drop them off Sunday before dinner.

This was very upsetting since it infringed on my free time and I was afraid it would negatively affect the children. After realizing that his inconsistency was a ploy on his part to use the kids to keep me from going out on dates, I was furious. Knowing full well that being angry would not get results; I decided to handle him with as much *divine decorum* as possible. At the time, I was more than willing to admit not being perfect with my approach on subjects such as this. So I requested guidance, meaning, I asked for a higher part of myself to chime in and offer some advice. It was the very beginning of my understanding of the **Positive Manipulation** process, but it proved to be a landmark event.

After spending time ridding myself of antagonism and clearing my head, a thought occurred to me; if he understood just how much time I spent with the children versus how much he spent with them, would the disparity jolt him into reality? I posed the question one Sunday afternoon while he was dropping them off. "Do you realize that on a monthly basis, I spend about 600 hours either with our children or responsible for their welfare and you spend less than 60? That's just 10 percent of their lives."

His face noticeably paled. When he heard the inequality put to him in a logical, unemotional manner, something snapped and his entire demeanor changed. As he dropped his guard, I went on to remind him of stories he told me about his own childhood and how he grew up without his dad around.

Soon after hearing my mathematic comparison, his behavior changed drastically and he started seeing the kids routinely. Years later, our roles reversed and while I was busy earning money to provide for them, he was the one going to the basketball games and showing up for "Meet the Teacher" night. He inadvertently learned from that lesson not to use the children, and I learned a better way to handle our co-parenting issues.

In this case of **Positive Manipulation**, my ability to drop my anger and resentment towards him for trying to control part of my life led to a clear and concise wakeup call he could understand and accept. If I didn't **Positively Manipulate** my own negativity, however, the idea of showing the difference in hours per month would have never come to me. Instead, I would have barked something like, "I can't have a life because you're not sticking to the schedule!" That statement would have challenged him to a verbal dual that would have escalated into a screaming match. And guess what? In the end, the kids would have never gotten any benefit.

ALWAYS THINK OF THE CHILDREN FIRST

Whenever there is any reason to question our behavior or that of our former spouse, our first query should be, "how is this going to be perceived by the kids?" In asking this question, we stop ourselves from being selfish and instantly become selfless. No matter what info we need or what money we want, until they are adults and can fend for themselves, children should never be used as the means to get anything. They are innocent by-standers in our drama and don't need more anguish to contend with. They need each home to be a safe haven, and if that is not possible, they need to at least be protected from added pressure either parent can knowingly, or unknowingly, inflict on them.

SPY KIDS

One of the worst forms of emotional abuse and negative manipulation on a child is espionage. If you believe your children are being used as spies, and you know their other parent will not stop, it may be beneficial not to say anything and decide to keep your private life completely hidden from your children in the future. If you ask them to not go back and talk to the other parent, it may instigate just as much apprehension as your ex did by asking them to spy in the first place. If you are the person who is making your child learn to spy, think twice! The knowledge you might gain will never compensate for the alienation you will experience, and in the end, the info you receive may hurt more than help you.

RITA'S STORY

Rita came to me as a client soon after she used her 20-year-old daughter to spy on her future ex. She suspected he had cheated on her (hence his reason for leaving the marriage) and she was obsessed with wanting to know about any other woman that might be in his life. She constantly questioned her daughter Teresa about her father's whereabouts and spending habits and then, finally, even asked her to play secret agent and check credit card bills at his apartment. Teresa begrudgingly agreed.

On her next weekend visit from college, she waited for her dad to leave for the gym and began to go through the papers on his desk. After looking through the previous month's statement, she found a hotel bill, airfare for two, and all kinds of eateries and activities listed, including a purchase from a jewelry store. Wanting to know more, she rifled through drawers and discovered pictures of him, arm in arm and vacationing with a woman she had never seen before.

Teresa, crying and unsure of how to handle the news, picked up the phone, but couldn't bring herself to dial. Should she tell her mother? Should she lie? Was her father going to marry this person? Was this woman going to be her new stepmother? Was this the affair that had broken up their family? She decided to call, bringing herself to expose what she found. Needless to say, after that conversation, both mother and daughter were completely traumatized.

Rita was always incredibly close with her daughter and they considered each other a best friend – which, by the way, is a very unhealthy position for any child of divorce to be in. Unfortunately though, a line was crossed. Realizing her daughter's dreadful reaction, Rita was guilt-ridden and devastated and vowed never to do it again. The pain associated with truth is sometimes too much to bear for an adult, so imagine what it can do to a child, even a grown one. At that point, her father was keeping his relationship to himself, knowing it would hurt his daughter (and his ex) emotionally. By pushing for answers, Rita put her daughter through psychological distress that was unnecessary. No one came out ahead on this one.

I know what it feels like to be spied on, stalked and have my privacy invaded. It was such a feeling of invasion to have someone peek through my personal items, such as poetry I wrote or cards I received from gentlemen I dated. It felt no different than being robbed, and I am sure it is just as much a crime. For those separated or divorced people out there who believe you are going to satisfy a deep need inside yourself by breaking into your ex's e-mail or voicemail account, or maybe calling credit card or cell phone companies, ask yourself if you are ready to deal with the evidence you dig up. If you are desperate enough to use your children to help you in this scavenger hunt, are you ready to deal with the repercussions and guilt you are going to instigate? Last question: If the tables were turned and your personal items and papers were sifted through, would you have mercy and show grace, or would you be livid at even the thought? Never mind. I think we all know the answer to that question.

SPEAKING OF BEST FRIENDS ...

Sometimes parents become so lonely during the divorce process that they rely far too much on their children for comfort, friendship and companionship. Playing the role of best friend can cause angst and turmoil as the child tries to figure out how to act, who to help, or worse, who to protect. Jimmy was only four when his parents divorced and his mother didn't handle it well. Turning to alcohol for support, she would get drunk each night and rock him in her arms, babbling on and on about how he was all she had left. Needing to have someone to care for her now that her husband was gone, she wanted to ensure little Jimmy's new position as man of the house. Unfortunately, this mother was creating the perfect scenario to raise an abuser. Jimmy would grow up filled with resentment for the role he had to play in his mother's life, but instead of taking it out on her, the woman he was forced to care for, he married and took it out on his new wife. Making a child of divorce into a best friend is dangerous and the repercussions can fill an entire book. Suffice it to say, our children are our responsibility to take care of, not the other way around. We need to constantly bear in mind their role is to be a kid, not a comforter.

REMEMBER WHO YOU ARE DEALING WITH

If we can keep in mind that our children are not our possessions, we will treat them with the same respect we expect them to give to us. Kahlil Gibran reminds us so eloquently in "The Prophet" when he wrote:

ON CHILDREN

And a woman who held a babe against her bosom said,
Speak to us of children. And he said: your children are not your children.
They are the sons and daughters of life's longing for itself.
They come through you but not from you,
And though they are with you yet they belong not to you.
You may give them your love but not your thoughts,

For they have their own thoughts.
You may house their bodies but not their souls,
For their souls dwell in the house of tomorrow,
Which you cannot visit, not even in your dreams.
You may strive to be like them, but seek not to make them like you.
For life goes not backward nor tarries with yesterday.
You are the bows from which your children as living arrows are sent forth.
The archer sees the mark upon the path of the infinite, and
He bends you with his might that his arrows may go swift and far.
Let your bending in the archer's hand be for gladness;
For even as he loves the arrow that flies,
So he loves also the bow that is stable.

"It is easier to perceive error than to find truth, for the former lies on the surface and is easily seen, while the latter lies in the depth, where few are willing to search for it."

Johann Wolfgang Von Goethe

COMMANDMENT IX
THOU SHALT SEEK TRUTH, ALWAYS

There is a right and a wrong way to do things, but many of us don't remember that there is also an in-between. Many divorcing people forget that there is a symbiotic or mutually beneficial way to handle every situation. Go into a discussion hoping to make the other person happy and guess what? You both reach your goals and both end up satisfied. This rule is most important when you have been terribly hurt by infidelity, alcoholism, gambling or worse, and you believe you are the one in the most pain. Emotions can skew your reality! I can't repeat this statement enough. Revenge, getting even, or getting everything will never make you feel better, irrespective of what Ivana Trump says. Peace within yourself and your new household should be your ultimate goal.

BECOMING A TRUTH SEEKER

In seeking the real truth, understanding how to create an altruistic goal is the most important aspect. In other words, you are now part of a divorced family. There should never be a "what is good for me" thought in your head. You are a "we," and you have been since the day your children were born. As the saying goes, get used to it. You have to repeatedly check yourself and ask, "Are these emotions based on reality and are they helping or hurting my loved ones?"

Why am I being so tough considering many of us may not even want to be divorced? Because we got married, we had children and then our marriages ended. No matter who did what, we are living in separated but united family units, as crazy as that sounds. More than ever, we can't just think of our own needs. Instead, we need to keep thinking about what is good for EVERYONE, and as soon as we do, the symbiotic (and truthful) solutions will come to us.

YOU CAN HAVE YOUR CAKE, BUT DON'T EAT IT

I have a saying, "Never *deprive yourself of anything. Instead, change your mind about what you want.*" By this I mean, don't think you aren't getting what you want just because a situation you are in doesn't come out exactly as you first envisioned it. Sometimes, we deprive ourselves of what is good for us because we don't want to give up what *feels* good to us. I usually use this phrase when speaking about food, but it applies to all of life. To help you understand, use this analogy: If you decide to go on a diet then you must give up highly caloric food. You might feel deprived at first of, let's say, chocolate cake. Decide however that you want an incredibly fit and svelte body and now, if you eat the cake, you will be depriving yourself of a new healthy physique. Which one do you want to give up? Which is more important to you?

I know this is going to sound unsympathetic, but as adults, we need to act responsibly and sometimes we don't like the direction that sends us in. We should always do what is right, truthful, and even heroic because our children should always come first, but do each of us do that? Clients ask me, "Does this mean that I have to give up everything that I want?" My answer is, "No, it means that you need to start *wanting* what is right for everyone instead of just wanting what is right for yourself." If you make it a goal to always do what is best for the family, and you achieve this goal, then aren't you getting what you want? So ultimately, there is no deprivation, right?

Dr. Wayne Dyer says over and over in his books, *"When you change the way you look at things, the things you look at change."* Alter, influence, or simply change *(Positively Manipulate!)* your mind about what you want and look at each circumstance from a multi-faceted perspective. If it is good for the children, your ex and yourself, then soften your view of what is happening in your life and consider it to be the best solution.

TRUTH BE TOLD

Truth is not just a spoken word. It is also the ability to discern right from wrong. Negotiations, discussions of assets, bartering of time and holidays, these should all be done under the heading of truth. No emotions, just the facts, and two people can always find a happy medium. Since all humans perceive life through their own experiences, hurts, pains, joys and sorrows, how can anyone rate a situation? Fairness is relevant. One may think a father without custody should have more holidays. Another may think a woman with custody should be allowed to change her weekend schedule at will so she can have more flexibility. Who is right? The answer is, there is no appropriate answer. But there is truth, and with the right goals, intentions and altruistic motives attached, you can always find it.

MALCOLM'S DILEMMA

Malcolm, a divorcing father, complained about his ex wanting him to take the kids on an off weekend. Even though he had no plans for that weekend and was just days before complaining to me about not seeing his kids enough, he denied her the switch. I asked why. It was the "principle of the thing" as he put it. I asked him to look at the truth in the situation. He didn't understand my request, so I prodded and pushed the issue. I said to him, "Didn't you tell me just a short time ago that you love spending time with the kids and wanted to have *more* time with them?" He said yes.

I held up one finger and said, "Truth 1. Now didn't you also tell me you had absolutely nothing to do this weekend and are having issues lately with being alone?" He nodded his head and said yes again. I put up a second finger, "Truth No. 2. Okay, now tell me the real reason why you said no." He thought for a moment and went on to confess it was because his ex-wife was going away for the weekend with her new boyfriend and he was jealous. I raised my hand and gestured with three fingers. "So now we have our third truth!"

"Malcolm," I said, "If there isn't a legitimate reason why you shouldn't take the kids and there are three truths or reasons why you should, can't you turn this around?" After some soul searching we concluded that he really wasn't jealous of the new boyfriend but instead he was jealous of his ex-wife's ability to move forward in her life and in finding someone to share it with, because, to date, he could not. I asked him to use the emotion he felt and transmute it into something worthwhile. That prompted him to be open to a potential compromise, and we came up with a new rule he could pitch to the mother of his children. He suggested that if she wanted him to take the kids on an off weekend, the schedule would need to stay status quo the following weeks. So in essence, he now had three weekends in a row with them and that made him feel more in control instead of being used.

TRUTH ALWAYS CREATES POSITIVE ENERGY

When it comes to situations like this, it should be noted that there is always an energy attached to untruths. As physicist Milo Wolff says, *"Nothing happens in nature without an energy exchange. Communication or acquisition of knowledge of any kind occurs only with an energetic transfer. There are no exceptions. This is a rule of nature."* When Malcolm said no to switching weekends, he gave a lame and false excuse. That sent out a negative current and caused a rift in the relationship with his ex. Although she didn't know whether or not he was lying, she could feel the negative vibration the lie caused. This always leads to more and more mistrust and discord.

In Dr. Dyer's book, "Excuses Begone!," he tells of his research into what is called "Memes" – it rhymes with teams – that have no physical properties in the body, but are actually thoughts, beliefs and attitudes in your mind that can spread to and from other people's minds. If this is true, imagine what harm can be done when we lie? It is imperative that we always interact with others, most especially the father or mother of our children, with truth and honesty in our hearts.

IS THERE A REASON WE ARE SURROUNDED BY WATER?

Negativity, like an untruth, resonates from our bodies. We are all connected by the same energy and give off vibrations that can be felt by one another. I have a theory that this activity is done through our fluid. I HAVE NO SCIENTIFIC EVIDENCE TO PROVE THIS! But hear me out anyway. One day, I was watching a show about dolphins and how they can communicate with each other from miles away. I started to think, could it be that humans are just like dolphins, but that water works for us from the inside out instead of the outside in?

After asking this question, I came upon the movie "What the Bleep Do We Know." (A great view if you can follow it. I have watched it about 16 times and still can't absorb it all.) There was a segment in the film expressing the opinions of a scientist named Masaru Emoto. He believed that water could be manipulated by negative and positive energy so he went on a mission to prove it. In the movie, he showed how he could write positive messages, like "I love you" on a glass holding plain, ordinary water. Then by freezing the water, he could capture and photograph its crystallized molecules. He also did this using negative phrases and words like "I hate you" to prove there would be a disparity among the crystals.

The results were amazing! Water crystals formed by the positive phrases were beautiful and distinct, almost forming their own language. Conversely, the negative phrases produced ugly, ill-shaped, almost non-existent crystals. The outcome astounded me and made me realize just how on track I may have been hypothesizing about water as a communication tool. Mr. Emoto truly believes that water has intelligence, and why should we doubt this? Is it too hard to believe that we may be the less intelligent life form on Earth? Aren't we consummated in water, then spend nine months surrounded by amniotic fluid? We are made up of over 80% liquid. We need it to survive. In fact, the only substance that trumps water is air. We emote with water through tears of joy and sorrow. When you think about it, why would we have the need to cry? We can lubricate our eyes without actually creating emotion. Ever think that crying is water's way of saying, "Here I am, emotionally *expressing* myself!" Okay, this sounds flaky, but do we really understand all there is to know about our bodies and how they communicate with one another or for that matter, the Earth?

After viewing this movie, I started to relate how we resonate energy, how I always know when someone is lying and how I "feel and sense" untruths even when I don't know any circumstances. Although I may be more in tune with these sensations than most, EVERYONE can feel lies. It may come across as discomfort, mistrust, or maybe even just a question mark in your head, but it is there. When we tell or hear an untruth, it is no different than the ugly words Mr. Emoto wrote on the water glasses. Our bodies will react, and then our minds will kick in and possibly come up with a scenario to match the emotion we are feeling. Most often, we negatively manipulate those emotions into more drama that may not be based on reality at all … and so the saga continues, over and over and over again.

OVERCOME YOUR OWN NEGATIVITY USING *POSITIVE MANIPULATION*

When it comes time to manipulate a thought or emotion, think about flipping the switch on those dark, negative thoughts and feelings so you can bring light and positive awareness in. Sri Chinmoy calls this our Inner Sun. In his book "The Wings of Joy," he writes about a great Emperor who ponders over a consistent thought about light. He asks his minister, *"Birbal, for a long time I have been thinking of one question. I am sure you will be able to answer it. We see everything clearly in the sunlight, but is there anything that cannot be seen even with the help of the sunlight?" Yes, Your Majesty,"* Birbal replied. *"There is something that cannot be seen in the sunlight. Even the sunlight fails to illumine it." "What is it Birbal?" "Your majesty, it is the darkness of the human mind."*

What Birbal could not answer however is how we will know, undoubtedly, what is coming from the dark and what is coming from the light. He tells us we should be continuously bringing in our inner sun. Instead of constantly giving in to our discomforts and negative emotions, we should always be seeking the truth in all our exchanges with our ex-spouses. If we do this, we give the gift of healing to ourselves and the marriage. Why is it so important to heal the former marriage? Because you want to extract every memory of each relationship in your life and make it into a wonderful lesson you can grow from. And when children come from that union, it should be even more crucial to consider it *meant to be*. If we don't accept the meant-to-be factor, we challenge the love in the union our children were created with and that invalidates their existence.

The ***Positive Manipulation*** process becomes imperative to keep this rule enforced in your life. No matter what you experience, your questions to yourself should be, "Is my perception of what is going on coming from a light or dark side of me? Where is the truth in this situation? Is what I am feeling real? Could my negative reaction be from my own issues? Am I open to hearing the truth? Is there a lesson being shown that I can learn from?"

PAM AND TODD

Todd was a great father and tried hard to please his wife throughout their marriage. Unfortunately, Pam had many emotional factors to contend with, including Bi-Polar Manic Depression. No matter what Todd did, he was never going to win against this disorder. He felt his only choice was to divorce her and hope that he would have a more positive influence on the children if he became healthier and stronger away from Pam's constant abuse. Although he had much to complain about, he instead decided to seek out reasons for Pam's behavior so he could understand her illness. Most people would not go through this after separating. Todd, understanding how important it was to encourage a healthy relationship with their mother, wanted to keep his children sound and his family unit intact, irrespective of how badly her abusive actions affected them.

In searching for the truth about his ex's BPD and the part her violent, alcoholic father played in creating her inner turmoil, Todd learned all he could about this illness and the erratic behavior it caused. He realized that he was divorcing a sick woman and if she had cancer, or any other disease, he probably wouldn't have left her. This realization alone helped him to see her in a different light – or should we say truth? Part of this condition was not her fault and was due to many biological imbalances and environmental causes. Of course, he still had to leave her because she refused to get help or treatment. That alone makes it impossible to keep the marital contract in force. One sided marriages never work, and understanding this, he was able to facilitate a better, less stressful separation period. But something even better came from the research; he was also able to start the process of healing from the cruelty he endured. By seeking the truth to help her and his family, he helped himself and took responsibility for his participation and his enabling of her behavior. He sought assistance through group therapy and located a spiritual advisor who eventually guided him past his negative emotions and challenges.

It wasn't long before he let go of the guilt he felt for leaving Pam, the self loathing for allowing himself to tolerate such turmoil and his resentment of her treatment toward the family. He took the steps to manipulate all the useless energy into that of love and forgiveness. All became clear, and as he got stronger, his place as head of the family strengthened as well, helping the children to cope with their mentally ill mother. The truth, as we say, set this family free of negativity. Even though Pam may never recover or acknowledge her participation, and the children may live with difficult issues for the duration of her life, they will always know their dad was supportive and not judgmental of their mom, in addition to always being there for them.

ALL IS WELL THAT ENDS WELL

Irrespective of how a marriage starts out or ends, there can still be healing if we seek out truth. Each and every one of us ALWAYS has a participation in the demise of our marriage. As long as we seek out that participation, we can heal ourselves and more importantly, ease up on how we feel about our former spouse. This in and of itself is freeing and will change the energy between the two of you. Eventually, if you are not exhibiting negative energy toward your ex, he/she has nothing to grab onto. Their behavior will change accordingly when you don't respond to their negative energy any longer.

In Richard Brodie's book "Virus of the Mind, I found a passage that gives great advice to truth seekers: *"One useful way to try out flexing your point of view is to take advantage of any disagreement you have with anyone. Instead of trying to win the argument or backing off from the conflict, try as hard as you can to see things from the other person's point of view. You'll know you've succeeded when the person you were arguing with says "Yes! That's exactly what I meant!" In fact you may even find that all the other person wanted was to be understood."*

EVEN THERAPISTS NEED HELP TO SEE STRAIGHT SOMETIMES

My uncle is a psychoanalyst and author of several books. He is well known in his field and has many followers. One day years ago, we were having a discussion about his ex-wife and her "stubborn attitude" about paying for half of their son's psychotherapy bill. "How can she refuse her own child his need for therapy? What kind of mother is she?" I looked straight at him and said point blank, "She isn't depriving him of anything. She knows full well that you, as a therapist yourself, will take him no matter what. She knows you will pay so she isn't withholding or taking it out on him. She is just not paying you."

He was dumbfounded that he didn't see it himself. We become so close to our own issues it becomes difficult to see truth. Believe it or not, knowing the truth lessened his angst towards her. He realized she wasn't a bad mother, just a bitter divorcee. This helped him to move forward with an understanding that they were still co-parents, but there was a very strong need for forgiveness of the marriage and each other. In the future, he would handle issues differently knowing the truth of the matter.

CAN YOU SEE CLEARLY NOW?

With the deep emotions attached to leaving your spouse, is there ever an opportunity to see clearly during the divorce? Chances are, whatever issues arise, they are padded and loaded up with all kinds of feelings unless we take the time to evaluate and rid ourselves of what we are carrying that is not necessary for our happiness or well being. Emotions are powerful and not always negative. We need them in order to survive. Fear keeps us safe, anxiety gives us empathy, grief keeps us from making mistakes over and over and anger gives us strength and clarity. But when we allow these emotions to rule or dictate our words and actions and continually invade our thoughts, they should now be considered compulsions, not healthy outlets.

In his book "Awakening the Energy Body," Kenneth Smith states, *"The idea is that the world we perceive is based on interlocking thoughts that form a grand composite. What we think the world is becomes a self-fulfilling prophecy where we verify our own thoughts day in and day out. The trick, then, is to stop thinking ... at least long enough, and regularly enough, to allow new perceptions to enter into our conscious world, to allow new thoughts to form, and then to repeat this time and again. It is therefore a means of discovering what exists, not what we think exists."* Because our body has a mind of its own, we have to continually question where thoughts, emotions, feelings and perceived notions are coming from. Our reality could be contrived by so many different aspects (remember the physical, emotional, and mental parts of yourself?) and during a divorce process, it is imperative that we constantly try and find truth in our circumstances.

Robert's Story

A very successful coaching client of mine called me one day to complain about his ex-wife. She had sent both their boys to a special school to enhance their SAT scores. When he got the bill, he lost his mind after seeing the dollar amount. It was tens of thousands of dollars. Furious at her for wasting his funds, but not wanting to cause a war before he found out the truth, he called me for advice. I quickly went on line and sought out the schools in the area and their price ranges.

During my web search, I discovered an article that talked about affluent families who spent small fortunes on SAT training. Apparently, people were convinced that if their kids aced an SAT, they would get into the best colleges and that would lead to a life of assured success. The bill amount he had told me about was right in line with what all the similar schools were charging.

I immediately called him with the news. "It would seem that your ex wasn't taking advantage of you." I went on to tell him about the newspaper article. "She fell into the same belief system as many other parents in the area have. I guess she just wanted to do what she thought was best for the kids and knew you had the money to do it." I finished speaking and waited for his response. There was nothing but silence on the other end of the phone. Suddenly I felt his energy disappear as if he was standing beside me one minute and left the next. Even from 100 miles away, I knew he was emotionally gone. "Hello, are you there?" He said yes and immediately excused himself, claiming to have a business meeting to go to. The disappearance of his energy confused me for some time. I kept thinking, "What was his rush? Did I say something wrong? Isn't it better to find out she wasn't just taking advantage of him?" Although we spent many hours over the next several years talking about various issues, we never spoke of this one again, but I couldn't let go of how he handled what I deemed good news.

It took some time for me to come to a conclusion about his behavior that day. Truthfully, I would never know the real crux of it, but I began to consider his true feelings about his ex. Having an affair that broke up the marriage, he was acutely aware of how his improprieties impacted the entire family. I believe he had at that very moment on the phone with me the vivid realization that he no longer had his wife as his champion. Through their life together, she "always had his back." He trusted her with much of his life, including money, but after his indiscretion, she was bitter and angry. The truth I revealed that day proved she wasn't trying to hurt him, but because of what he brought in to their lives, he might have suddenly realized that he lost the best part of his relationship with her; the comfort of complete faith in her intentions towards him.

Sometimes truth and seeking the truth hurts, but it is still the absolute best way to go through life. Although this event seemed negative at the time, he went on to face what his actions caused. The affair not only changed his marital status, but he lost a friend, liaison, soul mate and, more importantly, a trusted partner and confidante. When he decided to cheat, he apparently was willing to gamble on losing the marriage, but he may not have counted on losing the only person in his life that he ever trusted.

> **"Everyone is entitled to their own opinion, but not their own facts."— *Daniel Patrick Moynihan***

No matter what circumstance you face and how you feel about them, there is still a reality to be found; a truth that cannot be dismissed. Truth seekers temporarily put aside their human self so they can listen closely to their soul voice. Sometimes, when we are in tremendous pain and facing difficulty, that soul voice is small, almost inaudible, as the human voice is screaming in our ear.

It was some years ago that boyfriend No. 3 brought excruciating pain into my life, cheating on me during the entire relationship. I found out in time to not make any hasty decisions about my future, but not in time to rescue my heart from severe hurt and anguish. In an attempt to sort out my emotions, I wrote him an e-mail, or should I say, a printed diatribe. It started out, to put it bluntly, with venom. I held back nothing, ripping into this guy as if he were a piece of fabric I wanted to shred into rags. I knew I wasn't going to send it out to him as is, but it was cleansing to just spew and let it all out.

Night after night I sat for hours after work rewriting the email, each time editing and lightening it to produce a more loving outcome. Taking out a lot of the accusatory remarks and trying to *Positively Manipulate* my words into their best form, the e-mail began to take on a life of its own. I began to understand that by showing love towards him instead of anger, I was able to make excuses for his behavior and see just how bad off he was for doing what he did. It occurred to me that he was giving up a great relationship. We had much in common and had so much fun and laughs together. Since he was 14 years my senior, he had the proverbial "chippie" on his arm. Our children got along wonderfully, we were set financially and all seemed to be perfect. Why then, did he have the need to cheat?

I was led to research this question and in doing so, stumbled upon a website that was about sex addiction. While reading and answering the site's questionnaire, I came to the conclusion that he was definitely a sex addict and most probably an alcoholic. (Although I came to find later that he never really consummated the relationships he sought, but instead was constantly looking for validation that he could still attract anyone he wanted.) How could I have missed this? It didn't take long for this question to be answered because as I read over the survey once again, I realized I was answering yes to many of the questions as well! I was also an addict? I came dangerously close to being in that category. In my case though, it wasn't sex, it was love.

Seems that love and sex addiction are practically synonymous and in my attempt to keep the relationship, I overlooked all of the signs of it not working. After living through my marriage breaking up, then having Henry, boyfriend No. 1, cheat on me, and then No. 2, the semi-married man, putting me through two years of "I promise," I was desperate to believe that this was a loving partnership.

IGNORING THE TRUTH

Years ago, I set my goal in the form of a prayer by saying, "I want to attract my best partner." In doing so, a force and energy was sent into the Universe that was powerful enough to protect me from every wrong man I encountered. Because of my physical/emotional/mental state, however, I was not in tune with the small voice inside of me that was chanting warnings time and again when it was time to leave. Many stories I heard from this man were setting off alarms, and even though I sensed inconsistencies and asked many times, "That doesn't sound right. Are you sure you're telling me the truth?," he would never come clean. Instead, he chose to berate me for not trusting him and called me a "man-hater," using my past relationship failures as a reason for my lack of faith in him.

I finished writing that e-mail and wound up sending it, filled with love and forgiveness for his transgressions, reasons why he may not have been able to help himself, along with a detailed acknowledgement of my participation. I was strong, but I laid out excuse after excuse for him, knowing full well he was human with lots of issues. After all, even though he hurt me, he hurt himself more by losing love in his life. He called soon after and admitted to much of his betrayal, knowing that I wasn't looking for admission, but instead, a mutual healing. We are still friends and have no animosity towards one another, but moreover, I view the entire association with him as a wonderful experience I grew from. The truth helped both of us move forward with a new direction and peace in our hearts. More importantly, I recognized the break up as being rescued from a really harmful relationship.

EXPRESS YOURSELF

Many people are fearful of writing their emotions on paper and more so in sending their feelings out into the world. Writing is therapeutic and can be done for your own benefit without it ever having to leave your desk or computer. I teach clients to express all their sentiments freely, and then we use the rewriting process as an exercise to learn how to *Positively Manipulate* their words. We always want to soften how we present ourselves, and sometimes using emotion instead of thought has more impact with less harm. For instance, when you want to tell someone they hurt you, you say, "I am hurt by what happened between us." Right away, this lets a person into your emotional state and it is non-threatening. If you instead say, "I feel that what you did to me was wrong and it was really hurtful," it sounds accusatory. The rule of thumb is to say "I feel ..." and then recite the emotion. I feel dread. I feel sorrow. I feel angry. I feel delighted. These are all emotions. When you veer from feelings and go into thoughts, you will probably put a 'that' in front of it and it will sound something like; I feel that you were mean to me. I feel like you never listen to me. I feel you can't communicate.

What you are really saying is, "I think you never listen to me. I think you can't communicate." Expressing your thoughts instead of your feelings can put the other person on the defensive. If you take the same thought though and make it come from your heart, you would be saying, "I feel sad and all alone when you don't listen to me." Changing to emotion gives the person you are speaking with the ability to respond to your needs and the incident without being challenged. Here is when the adage, "feelings aren't right or wrong" makes sense! You can argue about what a person is angry about, but not the fact that they are angry. Now listen to the positive response to that last emotion-filled statement: "I didn't know how being inattentive made you feel. I don't want you to feel sad and lonely."

Expressing yourself to an ex-spouse may seem impossible, but really it is not. More importantly, it is imperative to keep the lines of communication open so a successful co-parenting experience can be accomplished. Each single person raising a child or children has many challenges and those challenges should be shared and dealt with as a team. When you decide that the parental aspect of the relationship should stay in force for the children's sake, then using this kind of verbal or written communication is crucial.

> **"Remember that when you're in the right you can afford to keep your temper, and when you're in the wrong you can't afford to lose it."—Gandhi**

The energy of Truth is pure and also attached to love – and remember, your motive for seeking truth is love for yourself and family. It raises the volume on the soul voice high enough to set you free of the negativity you may be encased with. In my situation, a desire to know why boyfriend No. 3 cheated led to new truths about myself. I could have stayed angry with him forever and no one would blame me. I knew better though: Believing we are right because we were wronged confuses the real issue, which is, even if you are right, that may not change your circumstance or solve your problem. I ignored warnings and that was more of an issue than his cheating heart. Even though it was hard to acknowledge how love sick I really was, unveiling my truth led to an incredible healing. Because of boyfriend No. 3, I NEVER doubt my intuition or soul voice. We should all constantly investigate our participation in creating our own pain and daily ask ourselves if whether what we are feeling toward someone else is emanating from them or ourselves. This is what will continuously free our lives of negativity and help to keep us on our best-life path. As Sri Chinmoy so eloquently states, *"Love the truth: This is human illumination. Become the truth. This is divine illumination. You are the truth: This is the supreme illumination."*

"It is during the legal stage in the divorce process, perhaps more than at any other point
along the way, that divorce paradoxically provides the greatest impediment as well as
the greatest opportunity to experience the presence of God. When facing a situation that
can potentially bring out the worst in us, to transcend our negative impulses and do the
right thing is an act of holiness. It is a moment of being fully human, of giving flight to
what Lincoln called 'the better angels of our nature,' a moment of reaching out to God for
strength, a moment of bringing in Godliness into the world. This is the mitzvah of divorce."

Rabbi Perry Netter *Excerpted from "Divorce is a Mitzvah"*

COMMANDMENT X
THOU SHALT CONTINUE TO LOVE AND HONOR THY FORMER SPOUSE

Many of us use the divorce process to take what we can from the other person because we are so disappointed in how the relationship and our lives ended up. We regret time lost, we commiserate over the need to mend our broken hearts and we agonize over material loss. Once we make the decision to leave, we want to run, and the last thing on our minds is what we are planning on giving and doing *for* our ex, but that is what we should be thinking about if we want a healthy split.

Society treats marriage as a union, but divorce as a state of being. Why can't divorced couples still maintain their union? When children are present, why can't a marital contract change from a fiduciary, legal document into a soulful, spiritual connection as co-parents, instead of it always being the other way around? If the blood of each spouse was mixed and blended together forever in the form of a child, then why shouldn't the husband and wife's commitment to love hold out as long? I understand it is easier to write these words than to accomplish the task, but does that mean we shouldn't at least try?

In order to keep the marital vows, there are certain conclusions we must come to. First, it is important to constantly remind ourselves that we attracted a certain person into our realm and we made the decision to marry him/her whether they were right for us or not. Second, we all make mistakes and we all have participation in the demise of our marriage, albeit a small portion or large. Third, irrespective of our decision to leave a marriage, we can't leave our family. That responsibility will always be there no matter how far we manage to run, physically or emotionally. We can all agree that keeping the vows makes sense, but the question becomes, how do we do it? Would it help to understand where and how things went wrong? If we took ownership, understanding and appreciation in exchange for guilt, blame, and remorse, could we make love into the glue we need to stick together as a family?

WHAT GOD HAS BROUGHT TOGETHER, LET NO MAN PUT ASUNDER?

While trying to clear out old hurtful sentiments, it is helpful to do a little mental feng shui to help clear your head of certain not-so-useful belief systems. Since most of us got married under the guise of some religion, let's start with this age-old saying as our first refute: In reference to "What God has brought together," will someone please prove to me or better yet, show me in writing where God had anything to do with your wedding? In order to relieve guilt or anxiety about our choice in whom we decide to marry or why we divorce, our question should be, did God put us together or was it a purely human contrivance? It is my belief that most of us choose our mates unwisely, going by a physical response in our bodies rather than a spiritual connection. Candace Pert, a noted scientist, actually states that love may be no more than a bio-chemical connection between two people. If this is true, does soulful love even exist in most marriages? I believe we can attract a soul mate, life and karmic partner, twin soul, etc., but how do we know which one of these profiles fits? Are we ever sure if a person we have found is supposed to be the person we should spend the rest of our life with?

Loved the wedding. Invite me to the marriage. – God

When we are young, we are so driven by hormones, how can we discern a good match? Also, in our earlier years, we don't know ourselves and make choices based on what we *think* we want in a life partner. If we were to wait 20 years, an entirely different set of standards would emerge. And here is more food for thought: If we made the choice to marry based on hormones, who is to say that hormones didn't play a part in every fight we had or every decision we made during the marriage? I continually see men and women mutilating each other's self esteem because of the "shape" their own bodies are in. A man's testosterone levels dive at a certain age; he gets a whiff of an attractive woman's pheromones – which compensate his lack by sparking his dopamine – and poof! Immediately he throws caution to the wind and acts on the physical response within his body. Next thing you know, he is in a full blown affair, blaming his loss of attraction on his wife instead of his own lack of good body chemistry. A woman goes through menopause, is highly symptomatic, starts to feel self conscious about her new body changes, loses interest in sex, withholds it from her spouse and expects him to love her anyway. Don't blame me for stereotyping. This is what I see and hear every week. They are all too familiar scenarios, especially considering the American diet and the addition of so many harmful chemicals that wreak havoc on our hormonal balance. Add in addictions to drugs and alcohol, physical and emotional abuse, gambling, lack of money, mental illness, society's fascination with sex and what do you hope to get? With all these issues to consider, it is no wonder that marriages fall apart! My point is that the vows we made at the altar years prior were not made by the people we have become. Should we be able to leave an unhappy marriage with the understanding that the odds were against us, our bodies and our original intentions?

Again, I am not advocating divorce. Truthfully, I would like a shot at healing every marriage in America and I believe, with the right team, many impending divorces could be parlayed into thriving marriages. I have repeatedly expressed my belief that if you take vows and bring children into the world, you owe it to them, your spouse and yourself to try anything and everything before making the decision to separate. There is only one problem; I need willing participants. Do you want to give it that effort? If you do, do you have your partner's full commitment as well?

In the early 1990' when I attended a Retrouvaille weekend given by our church to try and save my marriage, they asked these questions:

- *Are there only two people to consider in this relationship with no third parties involved?*

- *Are both participants clean of addictions (substance, gambling, sex, etc.) or at least desire to be rid of any?*

- *Is there any physical abuse?*

- *Are both husband and wife committed to the relationship and willing to make it a priority even if they don't feel love anymore?*

- *Does each partner desire healing even if they may not know how to go about getting it?*

- *Is each of them willing to take responsibility for their own lives, individually, and do whatever is necessary to change what is not working?*

If both husband and wife do not answer yes to every question, there is little hope their marriage will work. And this is why we seek divorce.

GIVING IT YOUR ALL

On the day of my wedding, my great uncle came up to me and my husband and said, "I want to give you two some advice that has worked for me and my bride for 50 years. If you both give each other 70% of yourselves, neither one of you will ever be without what you need." I thought about what he said and the wisdom behind it for a long time after our wedding. For many years I tried to apply it. I got married in 1980 and that statement has stuck in my head and is the basis for all of my couple coaching to date. The problem with many marriages that end in divorce is that there is usually one party or both who cannot or will not give of themselves without receiving first. Dr. Wayne Dyer's book, "You'll See It When You Believe It", reveals "the wait and see" mentality that most people will see what they want *only* when they believe in it. This means that as soon as you believe in your desire and trust in your ability to bring it in, then what you desire will come forth and only then will you ever be able to see it. I feel it is the same with most couples. One party is always waiting for the other to give first before they will give back. Basically, they want to receive love before they relinquish it. "I'll do it if she does." "If he says yes, then I will." If both parties feel this way, though, everything stays the same and no goodness can ever be exchanged! What it comes down to is lack of faith in one another or the love they share. They need to *see* the behavior before they can *believe* it can exist.

Someone has to start first. Someone has to make the decision that they will get it back if they let go of all the anger, resentment, fear and all other negative emotions and replace it with love. One person has to get the proverbial ball rolling and have faith that the evidence of this profound, selfless gesture will be seen, every day, every moment of your child's life, irrespective of what comes or doesn't come back to you immediately.

READ THE CONTRACT

Need help in getting started? Here is some advice: If you relive the day of your wedding and try to remember how you *felt* about saying your vows, you will probably have a better understanding of why we need to keep the love flowing. When you stood there, earnestly pledging to honor and cherish, you may not have known intellectually how tough married life could get, but you still knew the odds were against you, and you did it anyway. There was something else at work, something bigger than yourself that led your body, mind and soul to the altar. It was an energy, a power, a force. It was love. Here is where we must now create the new paradigm and stop believing in the traditional views of divorce. Leaving your spouse does not have to be synonymous with hating your spouse. Abandoning the marriage does not have to be synonymous with destroying the family unit. And finally, breaking the marital contract does not have to be tantamount with breaking the marital vows!

I took heed of my great uncle's advice during my marriage. Again, I don't claim to be totally faultless, but I always tried to give. In fact, I gave until I was stripped of all I had and there was nothing more to hold onto. I finally divorced because I felt there was nothing I could do or say to help him and I needed to finally help myself. Divorce made me stronger, which says very little for the marriage. When we promise to love, honor, and cherish, it is with the thought that we should be getting it in return. When we say "for better or worse," that doesn't mean to always give the better and take the worst. "In sickness and in health" would intimate that we take care of our partner when they can't take care of themselves, not that one side has to take care of everything because the other side refuses to help themselves.

At the last hour of any marriage, we finally realize that we can only give love; we can't make someone love us. We can help someone change only if they want to change. We can lead by example, but we can't make someone do what is right. When all is said and nothing else can be done, we are only responsible for ourselves, and when one part of the marital contract is broken or not adhered to, we have the right to nullify its existence, but there is no contract of the heart. None that allows us a severance of the emotional ties we share or the children we created together. The only thing that contract allows us to do is go on with our physical life. What happens to the rest of our commitment to each other is up to us and the laws we create for ourselves.

A promise is a cloud; fulfillment is rain. – Arabian Proverb

Envision yourself making every day an opportunity to challenge your personality and show only the part of yourself that you would want to share with a best friend. Picture yourself as your ex-spouse's partner, and not an enemy, as you both create a tranquil and loving atmosphere for your kids. Visualize your children's faces as you praise your former spouse and tell them all the good traits he/she possesses. "You take after your father" or "you act just like your mother" should instill a statement of pride in your children, letting them know that even though you can't get along with their other parent, you made a good choice in marrying them and you still want to keep the vow to love each other forever. That can be a child's greatest gift and our most profound life lesson: that your marital contract may need to be rewritten, but the promise to love and the energy behind the promise can stay exactly the same.

TO THE FATHER OF MY CHILDREN:

When we stood in front of the altar of St. Hugh's church, I promised to do my best, but it was based on what I knew at that moment. Our situation changed, but I know now that the love doesn't have to. You and I are still together for a purpose, to raise our children. I never promised, though, that I would stick around until our unhealthy relationship destroyed either one of us. I don't want you or the kids to hold me to the promise I made to stay with you, physically, till death do us part. I will however, cherish you forever for giving me the most incredible kids anyone can ask for. I will love you for the traits that I admire and for the reasons I married you. I will honor you as the father you have become, irrespective of how I believe you should act. And I will always feel affection for you because you are a human being that is a product of your past, and I wish to recognize the beautiful soul you came to Earth with. These are the vows I know I can keep, now and forever. – D.

"We promise according to our hopes, and perform according to our fears."

Francois duc de la Rochefoucauld

EXCUSE ME, BUT I NEVER PROMISED YOU A ROSE GARDEN

Spending so much time coaching divorced people, I am exposed to many tales of woe and am consistently made aware of the monetary inequities that can sometimes occur. It makes me wonder, why do people go into a marriage thinking everything will always be cozy? As long as I can remember, there has been an almost 50% divorce rate. Why don't people prepare for the potential that they may be alone one day? This boggles my mind because even if one doesn't believe their marriage will end in divorce, there is always the possibility of severe injury or death. If you are married in this economic climate, even if you both agree that the mother or father should stay home with the kids, shouldn't the stay-at-home parent still be thinking of earning money or advancing their education?

"I'm a marvelous housekeeper. Every time I leave a man, I keep his house." – Zsa Zsa Gabor

Two tough questions I have posed at one time or another to both sexes: One, "What makes some women think that because they were born with a vagina they should be taken care of for the rest of their lives? And second, "Why do some men think they are being financially shafted because they have to pay money every month to help support the family they created? Although these statements sound like judgments, that is not my intent. Instead, consider them observations. It would seem there is an issue in this country with entitlement. Many people believe they deserve whatever they can get or take. When it comes to families, however, who ought to be entitled to what? Should our birthright be dictating our right to money in a divorce?

DESERVING OR DEMANDING?

My cousin is a fortunate woman, and by that I don't mean spoiled. She works hard as a stay-at-home mom and does a beautiful job with her home and children. Her husband and his family own a thriving business and do very well financially. Although she is privileged, she has remained surprisingly unaffected by their wealth. Still, she lives in an area of affluence where some pretty advantaged families reside. Many years ago she told me a story about her neighbor, Carol, who was being forced to get a job by her ex husband. "So," I asked, "what's the problem?" "Well," she said compassionately, "Carol doesn't want one." This answer didn't sit well with me. I asked her a few more questions about Carol's situation, thinking maybe I wasn't getting the full picture. Turns out Carol never had to work during the marriage and she wanted to keep it that way. Having to provide everything up until that point, her ex-husband decided he was done with it. To make matters even stickier, she was disregarding a clause in her agreement that stated her alimony would end if she was married to or living with someone else. "So let me get this straight," I said with a bit of an attitude. "She isn't working and won't even try to get a job even though her kids are well into their teens. She is secretly living with her boyfriend, and she still wants her ex-husband to support her?" With the evidence piled up against Carol, my cousin was still sympathetic, and the more she stuck up for her, the more my feet started to rise off the floor. Since I have always taken responsibility for my own finances, I have to admit there was more than a twinge of judgment I was trying to manipulate out of. At the time, I wasn't in tune with the source of my discomfort, but looking back it is easy to understand, I was looking at her through broken glass.

When my children were small, I always wanted to be one of those moms who didn't need to work. I give credit to the husbands that can afford to offer their wives the choice, but I never had that option. Raising my children and working during the marriage was difficult, but raising them and working as a divorcee was even tougher, especially since they were 3 and 12 at the onset of the separation. It would have been great to share more of the financial burden, have less stress, and feel comfortable about our future, but instead I had to rely on my own ability to earn. I really didn't *want* to feel alone on this mission; it just worked out that way.

My righteous scrutiny was coming from an unhealthy place for sure, but there were also shards of common sense mixed in with my broken view. Even if my life had been blessed with a wealthy husband, I can't imagine allowing myself to act like Carol, who pictured herself as a victim. And if I divorced a wealthy man who had enough to support the entire family, I don't think I would ever be totally dependent. What would happen to me and the kids if he died or his money ran out? It just didn't make sense that Carol would expect a constant tree of cash to pick from just because she married someone who did well financially. Don't stay-at-home moms who marry middle- and lower-income men work just as hard as stay-at-home moms who marry affluent men? Why does one deserve to keep her lifestyle exactly the same after a divorce while the other is forced into a radical change?

> **"She cried and the judge wiped her tears with my checkbook."**— Tommy Manville, 13-times divorced millionaire

My cousin and I never saw eye to eye that day, but recently I questioned her as a follow up. She told me that Carol's ex-husband did eventually bring her to court so the monetary support could be finalized. She was given a very large sum as a settlement, but she never got a job, and as my cousin explained, she "frivolously poured through all the money in just a few years". Now struggling and living in a small apartment, her future was uncertain. Obviously my cousin was no longer sympathetic and realized Carol hadn't taken responsibility for her own life or finances, expecting her ex to always be a source of income. Part of me wanted to feel justified for the initial response I had years prior, but there has been much healing since then. All I felt was sorrow for her plight. She initially had everything she needed to start her life over, including her youth, but it would seem she never made use of her time or resources.

INDEPENDENCE HAS ITS REWARDS

Although it was a tremendous struggle, the most incredible feature of my divorce experience was my necessity to create a career for myself. Having no specific skill, trade, or education except one year of secretarial school, I went forth into the world with nothing more than a car filled with a tank of gas, a few road maps of Long Island and a new suit. I had nothing concrete to rely on except my gift of gab. I used to jokingly say, "Have mouth, will travel."

Needing to earn a living, and a good one at that, I was forced to find strengths, qualities and skills I would never have realized if I stayed at home. My growth as an independent woman was sort of forced upon me because of the lack of money in our household, but it was ultimately such a gift to me and my children! Both kids have respect for what I have been able to amass from so little, and my daring nature instilled an incredible work ethic and desire to succeed in them. My efforts paid off as esteem and character builders that would not have been fostered by me staying home and acting entitled, or worse, helpless while collecting checks every month.

Working hard afforded us college, cars, computers and many of the staples and extras a household needs to prosper. Today, most divorced families

HAVE to bring in two incomes to survive since the weight on one person is far too great to bear. Having one provider would make co-parenting almost impossible if you include time away to work long hours, lack of emotional support from the over-worked parent and possible resentment for needing to be the only bread winner. Staying home may seem like the best scenario for the children, and when they are very young or there are other circumstances to consider, it may be the best choice. But may I offer some insight from my 30 years of parenting experience? Irrespective of the physical schlepping my kids endured being dragged from one day care to another, they learned so much!

Kudos to The Boys and Girls Club of America, because without them and their low-cost, reliable, expert care, I wouldn't have been able to calmly let go of my motherly bond so I could focus on clients and work. My children grew exponentially from their experiences in day and after-school care. They were exposed to so much of what life offers outside of school and home. Needing to relate and mingle with so many children and adults, they learned about relationships and the give and take that is needed to communicate with people on all levels. They were challenged and stimulated daily by playing different games and organized activities with diverse age groups, and they physically received more exercise than children who sit in front of the TV or computer after school.

Spiritually, my children are humble, but confident, neither one has a selfish bone in their bodies. Both have worked since the age of 14, and they are always looking for ways to give back by donating their time and expertise to the community. These are learned and acquired traits, and I acknowledge all the help I had in exposing them to what would assist them in becoming the beautiful people they are today. They will tell you, though, that it was my desire to become a better, stronger, more independent person that had such a profound effect on how they feel about their own careers. Even though it started out as a survival issue, my journey, with all its nuances, helped them on theirs. We only have one shot at raising them, and how we live *our* life and what we do as people has more of an effect on them than anything we teach them verbally. The saying is "monkey see, monkey do" not monkey say, monkey do.

Eggs and oaths are easily broken. – Danish Proverb

When marital contracts are nullified, we may not be able to expect other promises to be kept. Now is the time to understand and embrace where you have ended up on your exclusive journey. You have the opportunity to re-create yourself, to plant your own rose garden right where you are at this very moment, a unique patch of earth that you can cultivate using the incredible talents and skills that make you perfectly you. "Being born is your gift. Living life is your challenge. Being the best you can be is your choice." When I wrote this mantra it was to remind my clients of all that encompasses a lifetime – the past, the present and the future. We should not define any of it by the sorrows, but instead, go forth each day with a new, loving and forgiving version of those experiences. Soften your view of your past, take responsibility for everything you are experiencing now and grab hold of your dreams for the future. And if you take nothing else from this book, remember this: Divorce is not the rite to be right. It is not a situation of win or lose. It is not about getting away with something or doing or giving the least amount we have to give. Divorce should not be made into more than what it is – the legal conclusion of a marital journey. But remember, with every ending, therein lies a new beginning.

It is how and where we go from here that counts.

ADVICE TO KIDS, WRITTEN BY SAMANTHA B. AT AGE 15

"When I was in 7th grade I found out my parents were getting divorced. In 8th grade I found out the truth why. That was the worst night of my life. Finding out your parents are getting divorced is like a doctor telling you your relative has cancer. But finding out why is like getting the call that your relative died.

Parents are never easy to deal with, especially ones who argue. But if you can make it through a divorce you come out stronger. Going through this divorce I feel I have matured quickly and I became a stronger person. I can't say that it was easy because that would be a lie. But what I can say is that, sometimes you're better off with two separate peaceful parents than two parents who fight constantly. People would tell me that all the time and it wasn't until it was over that I realized they were right.

No matter what happens, never blame yourself if you're a kid; it isn't your fault. I tried that and it only made it worse. Your parents love you and want the best for you. Sometimes it doesn't seem that way, but they do. I was the oldest in my family so it made it hard on me to know more than my brothers and sisters did. I still know more than they will ever know, and I won't ever tell them.

Remember, it will get better, they love you, and if you have siblings like I do, being oldest means you should be a role model. And what does that mean? It doesn't mean hiding your feelings so you look brave. It means you do whatever it takes to protect them and make sure you all get through it."

TOOLS FOR YOUR JOURNEY

Alicia Boyd Spiritual Healer and Counselor: www.aliciaspiritualhealer.com

Candace Pert: *Molecules of Emotion, What the Bleep Do We Know*:   www.whatthebleep.com

Dan Millman: *The Laws of Spirit* www.peacefulwarrior.com

Deal With Divorce: *Emotional Effects of Divorce on Children*: www.deal-withdivorce.com

Dee Wallace: *Conscious Creation* www.officialdeewallace.com

Doreen Virtue: *Angel Therapy* www.angeltherapy.com

Dr. Bradley Nelson: *The Emotion Code* www.theemotioncode.com

Dr. Brian Luke Seaward: Error! Hyperlink reference not valid.   www.brianlukeseaward.net

Dr. Francine Shapiro: *EMDR: The Breakthrough "Eye Movement" Therapy for Overcoming Anxiety, Stress, and Trauma* www.emdr.com

Dr. Karl Menninger: www.menningerclinic.com

Eckert Tolle: *The Power of Now*

Ester and Jerry Hicks: *The Law of Attraction* www.abraham-hicks.com

Gary Zukov: *Seat of the Soul*

Jacques Weisel: *Bloom Where You're Planted*

Jamie Sams and David Carson: *Medicine Cards* www.medicinecards.com

Joel Osteen: *Your Best Life Now: 7 steps to living at your full potential* www.joelosteen.com

Kahlil Gibran: *The Prophet*

Kenneth Smith: *Awakening the Energy Body*

Lynn Grabhorn, *Excuse me Your Life Is Waiting* www.excusemecourse.com

Masaru Emoto: *Hidden Messages in Water* www.masaru-emoto.net

Mike Dooley: *Choose Them Wisely; Thoughts Become Things!* www.thoughts-becomethings.com

Milo Wolff: *The Quantum Universe* www.mwolff.tripod.com

Mitch Albom: *Have a Little Faith*   www.mitchalbom.com
Napoleon Hill: *Think and Grow Rich*   www.naphill.org
Perry Netter: *Divorce is a Mitzvah*
Phylameana lila Desy: *The Everything Reiki Book*
Rene Descartes: *"I think therefore I am."*   www.renedescartes.com
Retrovaille Website: www.retrouvaille.org
Rhonda Byrne: *The Secret*   www.thesecret.tv
Richard Brodie: *Virus of the Mind*
Richard Dawkins: *The Selfish Gene*
Sri Chinmoy: *Wings of Joy* www.srichinmoy.org
Thomas Keating: *Intimacy with God: An Introduction to Centering Prayer*
Tim Janis, Composer: *Music With a Mission*   www.timjanis.com
Wayne Dyer: The *Shift, Excuses BeGone, You'll See it When You Believe It*
www.drwaynedyer.com